Fundamentals of Credit Creation in Banking

Fundamentals of Credit Creation in Banking

Lalit Lilothia

CYBER TECH PUBLICATIONS
4264/3, Ansari Road, Daryaganj, New Delhi-110002 (India)
Ph.: 011-23244078, 011-43559448 Fax: 011-23280028
E-Mail: cyberpublicationsdelhi@yahoo.com
Website: www.cybertechpublications.com

FUNDAMENTALS OF CREDIT CREATION IN BANKING

Lalit Lilothia

First Edition 2010

Asian Offset Printers

Published by :

G.S. Rawat for **Cyber Tech Publications**
4264/3, Ansari Road, Daryaganj, New Delhi-110002 (India)
Ph.: 011-23244078, 011-43559448 Fax: 011-23280028
E-Mail: cyberpublicationsdelhi@yahoo.com
Website: www.cybertechpublications.com

Preface

In money matters, any amount over and above the lent sum was defined as usury or riba. The ill consequences of usurious lending—the ruination of individuals and families—were witnessed at the local level and therefore the community held the practitioners in contempt. But the need for capital and loans existed and, in the absence of alternative solutions, the usurious lenders became an indispensable component of the society. They also exercised invisible power over their clients' resources.

If the clients happened to be in authority, the power extended to other areas as well; the greater the client's authority the extensive the power of the lender. Lending and borrowing between humans has taken place since time immemorial. People borrowed and returned implements, animals, foodstuff, etc. from their friends, neighbors and relations. They returned the same after use or in the case of foodstuff consumed and returned the equivalent when they came into possession of similar stuff.

When money came into being people borrowed that too and returned. It was all on the basis of mutual help—the borrower today may be the lender tomorrow and vice versa.

As time progressed professional moneylenders appeared on the scene, and they demanded a "fee" for the use of their money. This fee is now called interest, but till a few centuries ago it was called usury. In Islam, interest or usury, which in Arabic is called riba, is prohibited. Demanding, receiving, paying, witnessing, and anything connected with these activities are all equally prohibited.

—*Author*

CONTENTS

1

Introduction

The people-banking relationship is now undergoing a radical change in the State with both sides appreciating a new their respective roles, capacities and approaches. In the process, a new healthy atmosphere of viable financing and responsible entrepreneurs is slowly but surely taking shape. As a matter of practical necessity the "credit planning" should be prepared as part of the Development Planning of the area, otherwise it amounts to cart before the horse and the baby is already dead before it is born. The consistency and functional unity should be the principal article of faith. Therefore much remains to be done-right from the level of Village Development Plan.

The structure of banking in the State is naturally the same as at the national level. The structure basically contains the following three types: Of the three components, the nationalized banks are the bigger player.

In Manipur in 1999 only 86 branches are found operating, some "nominally" and some "effectively". 16 belongs to the State Bank of India and its Associates. 41 are branches of the nationalised banks, 29 are branches of the Regional Rural Banks. 51 are operating in rural areas. 14 are operating in semi-urban areas while 21 in the urban areas.

The emerging irksome atmosphere of undesirable law and order prevailing in the rural and hill areas has largely occasioned the "sorry state of affairs" of gradual disappearance of banks. This is bad for the banks and worse for the economy.

Now we can broadly visualise the possible concern of the "limited" performance of banking sector in Manipur by having a reference to 1) Population per bank. 2) Credit-Deposit Ratio (C:D) and 3) Per Capita Credit. The population per bank is fairly high.

It is 28,384 in 1999 as against 8445 of Himachal Pradesh and All India Average of 15,070. One cannot expéct efficiency of service-delivery with large population. Secondly, the Credit-Deposit Ratio is only 41.7% as against 68.5% in Andhra Pradesh and 93% in Tamil Nadu. In other words, the extent of credit-deployment for every unit of resource raised is fairly low. Thirdly, the per capita credit was only Rs.693 in Manipur as against Rs.50,381 of Chandigarh and Rs.4,270 of kerala. What is possibly required at the programme of training on "Banking, Finance, Project Planning and Management".

The direct finance to the farmers could be Rs.91 lakhs. The direct finance and indirect finance to the Small Scale Units in Manipur in 1998 amounted to Rs. 70.91 crores of which Rs.14.62 crores was meant for the village and cottage industries. Finance is the key to investment and hence to the process of growth. Providing saved resources to others with more productive uses for them, raises the income of saver and borrower alike. Without an efficient financial system lending can be both costly and equally risky. Trade, specialisation of production, profesionalisation, savings, efficient use of resources and risk-taking which are cornerstones of a growing economy are duly stimulated and streamline with a well structured networking of financial institutions. In fact development of any economy demands a responsive financial system free from undue temptation for acting merely as "Profit Centre". It has to act as constructive agent for development. It has to act as partner of development. It has to act as resource mobiliser. It is, therefore, one of the basic economic infrastructures. It is therefore not a surprise that the quantum of direct finance to farmers and Small Scale Units in Manipur was also low.

The first concern in any developing economy is lack of efficient mechanism of mediation between highly organised financial institutions and highly unorganised private savers whose savings constitute the foundation of the financial market. We have to monitor and review this linkage from time to time. The constraints and loopholes have to be dully addressed and plugged promptly.

BANKING THEORY

Economists attempted to explain the nature of cycles in models that used banking as a link between capital markets and money. Banks, as we know them today, developed as two separate, apparently legitimate, business activities: banks of deposit or warehouse banking, and banks of circulation or financial intermediaries. Fractional-reserve banking combined these two types of banking institutions into one institution—a single institution offering both transaction services and intermediation services. "The claim he has acquired by his deposit is also a present good for him. The depositing of the money in no way means that he has renounced immedi- ate disposal over the utility that it commands" and "the note is a present good just as much as the money" To the extent that agents attempting to build up cash balances reduce their spending on assets or attempt to increase their sales of assets instead of on other present goods, time preference has increased (in addition to the increased preference for real cash balances). Saving has decreased, not increased. The rate of interest rises, and the share of resources used for investment declines.

With the development of a fractional-reserve banking system, credit and money creation became institutionally linked. The early developers of an indirect transmission mechanism made use of these institutional features in their explanation of the effect of monetary changes on the economy.

A major factor in this analysis is injection effects. The way money enters the economic system—that is the injection—affects the dynamic adjustment process. There are initially affected by the monetary disturbance change before the demands of those who receive additional money balances only as the effects of the monetary change spread through the economy.

These injection effects are important. This analysis, which is the foundation of Austrian business cycle theory, combines the theoretical proposition that injection effects matter with the empirical observation that these effects take place as the banking system extends credit.

These are standard arguments concerning financial intermediation. Banks are hybrid institutions that could only develop as the result of special privileges granted to banks by government. The activities of these hybrids are not pure intermediation. The critical economic issue is: Is credit issued by a fractional reserve bank financial intermediation or credit creation?

In the traditional direct transmission mechanism of the older quantity theory of money, how money enters the system is deemed irrelevant or of the second order of smalls.

Monetary changes alter real cash balances. Economic agents respond through Pigou effects. Aggregate demand is affected directly as agents alter spending on goods and services in response to changes in real cash balances. Keynes effects are also essentially helicopter drops. Aggregate demand is changed indirectly as portfolio adjustments alter market interest rates.

A major disagreement between Austrians and monetarist or monetary disequilibrium theorists centers on the importance of these injection effects.

Money is created as banks make loans. The initial impact of a money-supply change occurs in the market for credit. Monetary changes that originate through the banking system alter not just bank credit but total credit available in the economy. It is not change in the rate of interest per se that causes the demand-side changes, but the change in the rate relative to the equilibrium rate. Such a rate reflects the "ratio of the value assigned to want-satisfaction in the immediate future and the value assigned to want-satisfaction in remoter periods of the future. It manifests itself in the market economy in the discount of future goods as against present goods"

Credit creation will thus alter the money rate of interest relative to the equilibrium rate and disrupt the balance between the "supply and demand" for capital. It is only in this relative sense that the money rate of interest is of significance in regard to movements of prices. It can at once be seen that it is quite useless to try to demonstrate the existence of any direct relation between the absolute movements of the rate of interest or of the

discount rate and movement of prices. At the core of this Wicksellian mechanism is the concept of an equilibrium or "natural rate" of interest. But what is the natural rate?

This natural rate is roughly the same thing as the real interest of actual business. A more accurate, though rather abstract, criterion is obtained by thinking of it as the rate which would be determined by the supply and demand if real capital were lent in kind without the intervention of money.

The problem is that: Monetarist and monetary disequilibrium theorists feel that these initial effects are swamped by later real balance effects. The Austrian–Wicksell mechanism does not preclude real balance effects, whether Pigou effects or Keynes effects. If the monetary disturbance occurs through a fractional-reserve banking system, then these spending effects occur, if at all, later in the transmission process and are of less importance for dynamic adjustments. The real balance effects do provide an excellent explanation of an economywide reaction to a helicopter drop. Direct effects would most likely dominate the response to such an experiment.

Where there is no clearly identifiable injection point, or the injection effect differs with each monetary change, no general theory is possible, and the monetarist emphasis on long-run results may be the best the economist can do.

It adjusts the rate of interest on loans to the rate of originary interest as manifested in the discount of future goods." Credit creation temporarily suspends this adjustment process.

In the economic system of today, interest does not exist in the form in which it is presented by pure economic theory... The process of interest fixation, which is the basis of pure theory, never in fact follows the same course in a modern credit economy; for in such an economy the supply of, and demand for, savings never directly confront each other.

Loans are made in money terms and not in kind. The observable rate of interest

is a money rate, a "return on borrowed funds" called the money rate that was equal to the natural rate the normal or neutral rate. The natural and hence the normal rate would be the equilibrium rate, the "rate at which the demand for loan capital and the supply of saving exactly agree" But if it is an equilibrium rate:

We must now consider whether it is possible for credit institutions to maintain their rates of interest at any desired level, or whether they are obliged sooner or later, as the result of the operation on the money market of the forces of supply and demand, to come into line with the natural rate. The latter is the view generally held by economists. In principle they are perfectly right; but they usually omit to provide any clear account of the mannerin which the two rates of interest are brought together. The money rate of interest depends in the first instance on the excess or scarcity of money. How does it come about that it is eventually determined by the excess or scarcity of real capital? Classical economists presumed that the natural rate was the determining factor. The money rate would differ from the natural rate only if the supply of savings was not equal to the level of investment. Saving would exceed or fall short of investment as the banking system changed the supply of money and credit in such a way that saving plus the change in the money supply would equal the level of investment.

Only Mises developed an argument clearly explaining why and how credit creation takes place. One must be careful not to speak simply of the effects of credit in general on prices, but to specify clearly the effects of "increased credit" or "credit expansion."

Under-finance and failure to finance in time (lack of timely finance) have been a constraint. Out of 8771 Small Scale Units operating in Manipur 2707 (30.86%) are found sick. Out of 79,555 Micro-Enterprises, 74,402(93.52%) are running without profit. 85% are operating without power, and 25% without their own premises. The performance of the State Public Undertakings recorded a negative return on investment (ROI) of 34.38% in 1992-93. The compound annual growth rate of manufacturing sector in the state records a negative rate of 7.4% during the period from 1991-92 to 1996-97 (RBI). One finds lack of necessary optimum exercises including financial networking as one of the major factors. The Bank-Industry-Economy interaction needs a thorough review in the light of new imperatives of globalisation.

The recent development of Refinance Market in the country represents a sound central initiative to step up and possibly diversify the capital market. Because of the Debt. Trap being experienced in Manipur, it has not been possible to take fuller advantage of the new opportunity. Availability of opportunity is one while utilisation of the opportunity is another. For example, under the Schematic Lending of the National Bank for Agriculture and Rural Development, Manipur could get only Rs.37.30 crores (as on 31st March 2000) as against Rs.4529.83 crores of Maharastra. Under the Rural Infrastructure Development Fund Manipur ceased to avail of the "fund" after 1st Phase with only Rs.0.96 crores as against Rs.723 crores of

Andhra Pradesh (1st Phase + 2nd Phase + 3rd Phase + 5th Phase). Recovery is bad, hence, refinance is not possible. Initianal provision is not found for the same, hence refinance is not possible. The spiral of debt-burden stands in the way of taking fuller advantage of the refinance market.

The recovery-performance speaks of the efficiency and maturity of the financial sector. Because delay is costlier and interests amount over time. The recovery is fairly low in Manipur. It is less than 20% as against 63% All India Average. The recovery performance of the Manipur State Co-operative Bank could be only 4%, the lowest in the country. Lack of incremental income accounted for 60%, lack of proper facility to repay 31% and willful default 9%. This speaks of the lack of "pre-investment appraisal" of the proposed unit of investment. There are four other general reasons namely bad recovery climate, weak collateral's, Law and Order and low banking habit. The whole atmosphere has four other implications as well; a) larger providing b) low profitability and c) low eligibility and d) low ground level actual credit (leakages).

SOME CAPITAL RATIOS

Government controls and bank regulations related to fractional-reserve banking have generally been used to impose restrictive requirements on note issue and deposit taking on the one hand, and to provide relief from bankruptcy and creditor claims, and/or protect creditors with government funds, when banks defaulted on the other hand. Such measures have included:

1. Minimum required reserve ratios (RRRs)
2. Minimum capital ratios
3. Government bond deposit requirements for note issue
4. 100% Marginal Reserve requirements for note issue, such as the Bank Charter Act 1844 (UK)

5. Sanction on bank defaults and protection from creditors for many months or even years, and
6. Central bank support for distressed banks, and government guarantee funds for notes and deposits, both to counteract bank runs and to protect bank creditors.

DEVELOPMENTS IN THE EXTERNAL SECTOR

The growing appetite of Indian companies for global expansion was mirrored in outward foreign direct investment (FDI) from India which showed a significant increase to US $ 5.4 billion in the first quarter of 2007-08 as compared to US $ 1.1 billion a year ago. During the first quarter of 2007-08, gross invisible receipts comprising services, current transfers and income at US $ 31.4 billion amounted to nearly 90 per cent of merchandise exports, recording a year-on-year increase of 27.5 per cent. Software exports, travel earnings, other professional and business services and remittances from overseas Indians underpinned the strength of invisible receipts. On the other hand, invisible payments increased by 18.6 per cent, mainly on account of a surge in payments related to travel, business and management consultancy, engineering and technical services and dividend and profit payouts. On a net basis, the invisible account recorded a surplus of US $ 16.9 billion during the first quarter of 2007-08 as against US $ 12.4 billion in the corresponding quarter of the previous year. The current account deficit (CAD) amounted to US $ 4.7 billion, broadly the same as in the first quarter of 2006-07.

Net capital flows surged to US $ 15.3 billion during the first quarter of 2007-08 from US $ 10.6 billion a year ago. Net external commercial borrowings (ECB) inflows at US $ 7.0 billion were sizeable and accounted for 45.8 per cent of total net capital flows as compared with nearly US $ 4.0 billion or 37.5 per cent of net capital flows in the first quarter of the previous year. Net portfolio investment by foreign institutional investors (FIIs) turned around with inflows of US $ 7.1 billion during the first quarter of 2007-08 as against an outflow of US $ 1.8 billion a year ago. The impact of the reduction in ceiling on interest rates during January and April 2007 resulted in non-resident Indians (NRI) deposits recording a net outflow of US $ 0.4 billion in the first quarter of 2007-08, a turnaround from net inflows of US $ 1.2 billion in the first quarter of 2006-07. Inflows under American Depository Receipts/Global Depository Receipts (ADRs/GDRs) amounted to US $ 308 million in April-June 2007.

Reflecting the movements in current and capital accounts of the balance of payments, the accretion to foreign exchange reserves (excluding valuation) amounted to US $ 11.2 billion during the first quarter of 2007-08 as against US $ 6.4 billion a year ago. Taking into account the valuation gain of US $ 3.0 billion, the level of foreign exchange reserves amounted to US $ 213.4 billion at the end of June 2007.

India's external debt increased by US $ 8.7 billion during April-June 2007 and amounted to US $ 165.4 billion at end-June 2007. While multilateral debt registered a moderate increase of US $ 317 million, there was a marginal decline of US $ 417 million in bilateral debt. ECB increased by US $ 5.5 billion while there was an increase of US $ 1.0 billion in short-term trade credits. Valuation gains on account of the appreciation of the US dollar vis-à-vis other major international currencies added US $ 1.2 billion to the stock of external debt. The US dollar had a dominant share of 50.4 per cent in India's external debt whereas rupee-denominated debt had a share of 18.0 per cent. The ratio of short-term debt to total debt increased marginally to 7.9 per cent at end-June 2007 from 7.6 per cent at end-March 2007. The ratio of foreign exchange reserves to external debt was 129.0 per cent at the end of June 2007 as compared with 127.1 per cent at end-March 2007.

These developments appear to have gained ground in the second quarter of 2007-08. According to the DGCI&S, merchandise exports rose by 18.2 per cent in US dollar terms during April-August 2007 as compared with 27.1 per cent in the corresponding period of the previous year. Import growth was higher at 31.0 per cent as compared with 20.6 per cent in the previous year. Non-oil imports rose by as much as 44.3 per cent (10.9 per cent a year ago); oil imports, however, slowed down to 6.0 per cent (44.5 per cent), mainly on account of moderation in the price of the Indian basket of crude oil by 0.5 per cent during April-August 2007 (US $ 68.0 per barrel) as against an increase of 30.2 per cent during April-August 2006 (US $ 68.4 per barrel). On the other hand, oil import in volume terms increased by 18 per cent during April-May 2007 as compared with 13 per cent in April-May 2006. As a result, the merchandise trade deficit widened to US $ 32.5 billion during April-August 2007 from US $ 19.9 billion in April-August 2006. There are also indications of a substantial increase in remittances received from Indians working abroad as well as sustained resilience and growth in exports of software and IT enabled services.

Balance of payments data for the first quarter of 2007-08 released by the Reserve Bank at the end of September 2007 indicate a widening of the merchandise trade deficit on a year-on-year basis, sustained buoyancy in invisibles and sizeable net capital inflows which comfortably met the external financing requirement for April-June 2007 and also enabled a build-up of international reserves, fortifying the stability and strength of India's external sector. In US dollar terms, merchandise export growth was 17.8 per cent during April-June 2007 as against 23.7 per cent in the first quarter of the previous year. Commodity-wise data available from the Directorate General of Commercial Intelligence and Statistics (DGCI&S) for April-May 2007 indicate that exports of petroleum products, engineering goods and gems and jewellery together contributed 69 per cent of overall export growth as compared with 66 per cent in April-May 2006.

The growth of exports of primary products moderated to 7.1 per cent, mainly due to the deceleration in the exports of agriculture and allied products; exports of ores and minerals, however, showed a turnaround during April-May 2007. Exports of manufactures registered a growth of 12.7 per cent in April-May 2007 as against 12.2 per cent a year ago. While growth of exports of chemicals and related products moderated to 7.9 per cent as compared with 12.1 per cent, export of textiles and related products declined by 7.7 per cent as against an increase of 11.6 per cent. Merchandise import payments rose by 21.3 per cent during the first quarter of the 2007-08 as compared with 22.9 per cent a year ago. While crude oil import growth at 8.0 per cent moderated from 45.2 per cent, non-oil import payments increased by 47.4 per cent, reflecting the underlying strength of domestic demand. The main drivers of non-oil import growth in 2007-08 so far (April-May) were capital goods, iron and steel, gold and silver, pearls, precious and semi-precious stones, chemicals and metalliferrous ores and metal scrap. China remained the major source of imports in April-May 2007 accounting for 10 per cent of total imports and 14.8 per cent of non-oil imports. On a payments basis, the merchandise trade deficit widened to US $ 21.6 billion in the first quarter of 2007-08 from US $ 16.9 billion a year ago.

Available information points to a scaling up of various elements of net capital flows in relation to their levels a year ago and even in the preceding quarter. Portfolio flows have picked up strongly on account of FIIs, amounting to US $ 21.2 billion during 2007-08 (up to October 19) as compared to an inflow of US $ 0.9 billion in the corresponding period of 2006-07. Gross FDI inflows during April-July 2007 were placed at US $ 6.6 billion as compared with US $ 3.7 billion a year ago. Approvals for ECBs amounted to US $ 8.7 billion during April-June 2007 as compared with US $ 4.4 billion in the corresponding period last year. On the other hand, there were net outflows under NRI deposits of US $ 148 million in April-July 2007 as compared with inflows of US $ 1,585 million during April-July 2006. ADR/GDR issues by Indian companies amounted to US $ 2.3 billion during April-July 2007 as against an inflow of US

$ 1.5 billion in the corresponding period in the previous year. The foreign exchange reserves increased by US $ 62.0 billion and stood at US $ 261.1 billion on October 19, 2007.

The exchange rate of the rupee against the US dollar, which was Rs.43.59 at end-March 2007, appreciated thereafter to reach Rs.41.24 at end-August 2007 and strengthened further to Rs.39.51 per US dollar as on October 26, 2007. The rupee appreciated by 10.3 per cent against the US dollar, by 2.4 per cent against the euro, by 5.4 per cent against the pound sterling and 7.1 per cent against the Japanese yen during the current financial year up to October 26, 2007.

The exchange rate policy in recent years has been guided by the broad principles of careful monitoring and management of exchange rates with flexibility, without a fixed target or a pre-announced target or a band, coupled with the ability to intervene, if and when necessary. The overall approach to the management of India's foreign exchange reserves takes into account the changing composition of the balance of payments and endeavours to reflect the 'liquidity risks' associated with different types of flows and other requirements.

THE ANNUAL POLICY STATEMENT FOR 2007-08

GDP growth forecast retained at 8.5 per cent during 2007-08, assuming no further escalation in international crude prices and barring domestic or external shocks Inflation to be contained close to 5.0 per cent during 2007-08 while resolving to condition expectations in the range of 4.0-4.5 per cent, with a medium-term objective of inflation at around 3.0 per cent. Moderating net capital flows so that money supply is not persistently out of alignment with indicative projection of 17.0-17.5 per cent. Covering of 'Short-sale' and 'When Issued' transactions to be permitted outside the Negotiated Dealing System - Order Matching (NDS-OM) system.

Systemically important non-deposit taking NBFCs (NBFC-ND-SI) to be considered as 'qualified entities' for accessing the

NDS-OM using the Constituents' Subsidiary General Ledger (CSGL) route.

Reinstatement of the eligible limits under the past performance route for hedging facility to be permitted.

Oil companies to be permitted to hedge foreign exchange exposures by using overseas over-the-counter (OTC)/ exchange traded derivatives up to a maximum of one year forward.

Importers and exporters having foreign currency exposures to be allowed to write covered call and put options in both foreign currency/ rupee and cross currency and receive premia. Bank Rate, Repo Rate and Reverse Repo Rate kept unchanged. The flexibility to conduct overnight repo or longer term repo including the right to accept or reject tender(s) under the LAF, wholly or partially, is retained.

CRR increased by 50 basis points to 7.5 per cent effective fortnight beginning November 10, 2007.

Authorised Dealers (ADs) to be permitted to run cross currency options books subject to the Reserve Bank's approval.

ADs to be permitted to offer American options as well.

Working Group to be constituted for preparing a road-map for migration to core banking solutions (CBS) by Regional Rural Banks (RRBs).

RRBs and State/ Central Cooperative Banks to disclose their capital-to-risk weighted assets ratio (CRAR) as on March 31, 2008 in their balance sheets. A road-map to be evolved for achieving the desired level of CRAR by these banks. High Level Committee to be constituted to review the Lead Bank Scheme. Financial assistance to RRBs for implementing information and communication technology (ICT) based solutions. Working group to be constituted to lay down the road-map for cross-border supervision and supervisory cooperation with overseas regulators, consistent with the framework envisaged in the Basel Committee on Banking Supervision (BCBS).

Besides general market risk, specific risk, especially the credit risk arising out of deficient documentation or settlement risk to be covered under the supervisory process.

Action plan to be drawn up for implementation of National Electronic Clearing Service (NECS) with centralised clearing and settlement at Mumbai.

MONETARY DEVELOPMENTS

The Reserve Bank of India today released the document "Macroeconomic and Monetary Developments: Mid-Term Review 2007-08" to serve as a backdrop to the Mid-Term Review of the Annual Policy Statement for 2007-08 being announced on October 30, 2007.

The highlights of macroeconomic and monetary developments during 2007-08 so far are:

THE REAL ECONOMY

The Indian economy continued to maintain strong growth momentum during the first quarter of 2007-08, underpinned by sustained performances of the manufacturing and services sectors. According to the estimates released by the Central Statistical Organisation (CSO) in August 2007, real GDP growth was 9.3 per cent during the first quarter of 2007-08 as compared with 9.6 per cent during the same period in 2006-07.

The cumulative rainfall during the South-West monsoon season 2007 (June to September) was 5 per cent above normal as compared with one per cent below normal during the corresponding period of the previous year. The area coverage of kharif crops has increased during 2007-08 (as on October 12, 2007) with reported sown area of 104.7 per cent of the normal, which was about 3.1 per cent higher than the previous year.

During April-August 2007, the index of industrial production rose by 9.8 per cent as compared with a growth of 11.0 per cent recorded during the corresponding period of the previous year. The manufacturing sector registered a growth of 10.3 per cent during April-August 2007 on top of 12.2 per cent during April-August 2006.

During April-August 2007, the infrastructure sector recorded a growth of 6.6 per cent as compared with 8.3 per cent a year ago, with five of the six core infrastructure industries registering a deceleration. The electricity sector was the only sector which recorded a higher growth than a year ago.

The services sector continued to record double-digit growth (10.6 per cent) in April-June 2007. Leading indicators of service sector activity for April-August 2007 show that cargo handled at major ports and import cargo handled by civil aviation witnessed strong growth. Growth rates in commercial vehicle production, new cell phone connections, passengers handled by civil aviation and steel moderated during 2007-08 (April-August), albeit over a high base.

FISCAL SITUATION

Available information on Central Government finances for 2007-08 (April-August) indicates that gross fiscal deficit (as proportion of the budget estimates) was placed higher than a year ago. Revenue deficit (adjusted for profit on sale of Reserve Bank's stake in SBI) was 122.9 per cent of the full year budget estimates. Tax revenue remained buoyant, rising by 22.0 per cent over that during April-August 2006. Non-tax revenue (net of profit on sale of Reserve Bank's stake in SBI) registered a growth of 21.2 per cent during the same period. Aggregate expenditure (adjusted for acquisition cost of Reserve Bank's stake in SBI) increased mainly on account of sharp increase in revenue expenditure and plan capital expenditure.

Gross and net market borrowings (including 364-day Treasury Bills) of the Central Government during 2007-08 (up to October 22, 2007) were Rs.1,26,036 crore and Rs.75,363 crore, respectively, accounting for 66.7 per cent and 68.7 per cent of the estimated borrowings for the year.

During 2007-08 (up to October 22, 2007), the States raised market loans amounting to Rs.20,362 crore (50.1 per cent of gross allocation) through auctions.

Price Situation

Headline inflation generally edged up in major economies during the quarter ended September 2007 as compared with the previous quarter. Many central banks further tightened monetary policy during the second quarter of 2007-08 against the backdrop of persistent inflationary pressures represented by core inflation, especially in view of continued strength of demand, ample liquidity and possible pass-through from past and present increases in oil and other commodity prices.

Global commodity prices remained firm during the second quarter of 2007-08 led by food and crude oil prices, although there was some moderation in prices of metals during the quarter. International crude (WTI) prices crossed US $ 80 a barrel by mid-September 2007 and reached a historical peak on October 18, 2007 at US $ 89.5 a barrel, partly due to heightened geopolitical tensions in West Asia and the weakening of the US dollar. Food prices increased further led by wheat and oilseeds/edible oils, reflecting a shortfall in global production, decline in stocks and rising demand for non-food uses.

In India, inflation based on the wholesale price index (WPI) eased from 4.4 per cent at end-June 2007 to 3.1 per cent by October 13, 2007, partly due to base effects and negative contribution from fuel prices.

Pre-emptive monetary measures since mid-2004 accompanied by fiscal and supply-side measures have helped in containing inflation. Fuel group inflation turned negative beginning the week ended June 9, 2007 and remained so (-1.6 per cent) on October 13, 2007, easing from 5.0 per cent a year ago, reflecting the cuts in domestic prices of petrol, diesel and other fuel products in November 2006 and February 2007. Primary articles' inflation eased to 5.2 per cent on October 13, 2007 from 9.3 per cent at end-June 2007 and 8.1 per cent a year ago. Manufactured products inflation eased to 4.1 per cent on October 13, 2007 from 4.9 per cent at end-June 2007 and 4.6 per cent a year ago. Various measures of consumer price inflation were placed in the range of 5.7-7.9 per cent during August/September 2007 as compared with 5.7-7.8 per cent in June 2007 (and 6.7-9.5 per cent in March 2007). Consumer price inflation, however, remained firm during the second quarter of 2007-08 and continued to be above the WPI inflation, mainly reflecting the impact of higher food prices.

2

Liquidity and Capital Management for a Bank

INTRODUCTION

To avoid defaulting on its obligations, the bank must maintain a minimal reserve ratio that it fixes in accordance with, notably, regulations and its liabilities. In practice this means that the bank sets a reserve ratio target and responds when the actual ratio falls below the target. Such response can be, for instance:

1. Selling or redeeming other assets, or securitization of illiquid assets,
2. Restricting investment in new loans,
3. Borrowing funds (whether repayable on demand or at a fixed maturity),
4. Issuing additional capital instruments, or
5. Reducing dividends.

Because different funding options have different costs, and differ in reliability, banks maintain a stock of low cost and reliable sources of liquidity such as:

1. Demand deposits with other banks
2. High quality marketable debt securities

3. Committed lines of credit with other banks

As with reserves, other sources of liquidity are managed with targets.

The ability of the bank to borrow money reliably and economically is crucial, which is why confidence in the bank's creditworthiness is important to its liquidity. This means that the bank needs to maintain adequate capitalisation and to effectively control its exposures to risk in order to continue its operations. If creditors doubt the bank's assets are worth more than its liabilities, all demand creditors have an incentive to demand payment immediately, a situation known as a run on the bank.

Contemporary bank management methods for liquidity are based on maturity analysis of all the bank's assets and liabilities (off balance sheet exposures may also be included). Assets and liabilities are put into residual contractual maturity buckets such as 'on demand', 'less than 1 month', '2-3 months' etc. These residual contractual maturities may be adjusted to account for expected counter party behaviour such as early loan repayments due to borrowers refinancing and expected renewals of term deposits to give forecast cash flows. This analysis highlights any large future net outflows of cash and enables the bank to respond before they occur. Scenario analysis may also be conducted, depicting scenarios including stress scenarios such as a bank-specific crisis.

RISK AND PRUDENTIAL REGULATION

In a fractional-reserve banking system, in the event of a bank run, the demand depositors and note holders would attempt to withdraw more money than the bank has in reserves, causing the bank to suffer a liquidity crisis and, ultimately, to perhaps default. In the event of a default, the bank would need to liquidate assets and the creditors of the bank would suffer a loss if the proceeds were insufficient to pay its liabilities. Since public deposits are payable on demand, liquidation may require selling assets quickly and potentially in large enough quantities to affect the price of those assets. An otherwise solvent bank (whose assets are worth more than its liabilities) may be made insolvent by a bank run. This problem potentially exists for any corporation with debt or liabilities, but is more critical for banks as they rely upon public deposits (which may be redeemable upon demand).

Although an initial analysis of a bank run and default points to the bank's inability to liquidate or sell assets (i.e. because the fraction of assets not held in the form of liquid reserves are held in less liquid investments such as loans), a more full analysis indicates that depositors will cause a bank run only when they have a genuine fear of loss of capital, and that banks with a strong risk adjusted capital ratio should be able to liquidate assets and obtain other sources of finance to avoid default. For this reason, fractional-reserve banks have every reason to maintain their liquidity, even at the cost of selling assets at heavy discounts and obtaining finance at high cost, during a bank run (to avoid a total loss for the contributors of the bank's capital, the shareholders).

Many governments have enforced or established deposit insurance systems in order to protect depositors from the event of bank defaults and to help maintain public confidence in the fractional-reserve system.

Responses to the problem of financial risk described above include:

1. Proponents of prudential regulation, such as minimum capital ratios, minimum reserve ratios, central bank or other regulatory supervision, and compulsory note and deposit insurance,
2. Proponents of free banking, who believe that banking should be open to free entry and competition, and that the self-interest of debtors, creditors and shareholders should result in effective risk management; and,

3. Withdrawal restrictions: some bank accounts may place a limit on daily cash withdrawals and may require a notice period for very large withdrawals.

   Banking laws in some countries may allow restrictions to be placed on withdrawals under certain circumstances, although these restrictions may rarely, if ever, be used;

4. Opponents of fractional reserve banking who insist that notes and demand deposits be 100% reserved.

MONETARY AND LIQUIDITY CONDITIONS

Growth in broad money (M3), year-on-year (y-o-y), was 21.8 per cent (Rs. 6,41,464 crore) on October 12, 2007 as compared with 18.9 per cent (Rs. 4,66,603 crore) a year ago.

Aggregate deposits of banks, y-o-y, increased by 23.4 per cent (Rs.5,83,198 crore) on October 12, 2007 as compared with 19.2 per cent (Rs. 4,01,717 crore) a year ago.

Growth in bank credit moderated after the strong pace in the preceding three years. Non-food credit by scheduled commercial banks (SCBs) moderated to 23.5 per cent (Rs.3,77,759 crore), y-o-y, as on October 12, 2007 from 30.0 per cent (Rs.3,70,226 crore) a year ago.

Reserve money expanded by 24.4 per cent (14.9 per cent adjusted for the first round impact of the increase in the cash reserve ratio), y-o-y, as on October 19, 2007 as compared with 20.2 per cent a year ago.

Liquidity conditions continued to be influenced by movements in capital flows and cash balances of the Governments.

The Reserve Bank modulated market liquidity with the help of issuances of securities under the Market Stabilisation Scheme (MSS), operations under Liquidity Adjustment Facility (LAF) and increase in the cash reserve ratio (CRR).

The External Economy

India's balance of payments position has remained comfortable during 2007-08 so far. The merchandise trade deficit, on balance of payments basis, increased from US$ 16.9 billion in April-June 2006 to US$ 21.6 billion in April-June 2007. Net surplus on the invisibles account exhibited buoyancy during the first quarter of 2007-08, led by exports of software, business services and private remittances, and continued to finance a large part (78.2 per cent) of the merchandise trade deficit.

Despite large merchandise trade deficit, higher net invisible surplus contained the current account deficit (US$ 4.7 billion) during the first quarter of 2007-08 at broadly the same level (US$ 4.6 billion) as in the first quarter of 2006-07. The current account deficit was financed by capital flows which have remained large during 2007-08 so far.

During 2007-08 (up to October 19, 2007), net inflows by FIIs amounted to US $21.2 billion as compared with outflows of US $ 933 million in the corresponding period of 2006-07. FDI inflows were US $ 6.6 billion during April-July 2007 (US $ 3.7 billion a year ago). On the other hand, non-resident Indian deposits registered net outflows amounting to US $ 148 million during April-July 2007 as against net inflows of US $ 1.6 billion during April-July 2006.

During 2007-08 so far (April-August), growth of merchandise exports moderated, while imports posted a high growth rate. Non-oil imports registered high growth due to robust growth in capital goods. Oil imports registered a sharp deceleration from the strong growth recorded during the corresponding period of the previous year.

India's foreign exchange reserves were US $ 261.1 billion as on October 19, 2007, showing an increase of US $ 62.0 billion over end-March 2007 level.

The Annual Policy Statement of April 2007 emphasised the need for credit quality and orderly conditions in financial markets for securing macroeconomic and, in particular, financial stability while pursuing greater credit penetration and financial inclusion. In consonance, the Annual Policy Statement on Regulatory and Developmental Policies set out measures in terms of issuance of guidelines on derivatives; implementation of Basel II; restructuring of advances including advances to SMEs; differentiated bank licenses; bank finance to factoring companies; enhancement of disclosures; know your customer (KYC) norms/anti-money laundering (AML) standards; credit information companies; and convergence with international best practices. In this context, drawing up of a road-map for introduction of currency and interest rate futures was proposed along with ongoing liberalisation of foreign exchange transactions.

The First Quarter Review of July 2007 intensified policy monitoring in the context of high volatility in equity and currency markets. Banks, financial institutions and corporates were advised to be vigilant and well prepared with appropriate risk mitigation strategies to deal with significantly higher volatilities than before. It was indicated that contextually, financial stability would assume greater importance in the months to come.

Going forward, the Reserve Bank would continue to balance the development of a sound, efficient and diversified financial system that facilitates smooth transmission of monetary policy with financial inclusion in which satisfactory customer services are rendered by financial institutions/ intermediaries. Credible communication, adequate availability of information and a broad-based, participative and consultative approach will shape the conduct of developmental and regulatory policies in respect of the financial system.

The Mid-term Review of the Annual Statement on Developmental and Regulatory Policies focuses on certain key areas: new financial instruments and prudential requirements; liberalisation of foreign exchange transactions; strengthening risk management in banks; migration to Basel II; fine-tuning of supervisory processes in response to financial innovations and consolidation in the banking sector and business processes; ongoing development and integration of various segments of financial markets; and improved credit delivery mechanisms with specific focus on the developmental needs of agriculture and small and medium enterprises and inclusive growth.

This Review is divided into four sections:

FINANCIAL MARKETS

The Reserve Bank has consistently emphasised the importance of developing financial markets as well as operational flexibility for market participants in various segments in an environment secured by effective regulation and oversight.

The Technical Advisory Committee (TAC) on Money, Foreign Exchange and Government Securities Markets has provided valuable guidance to the Reserve Bank in the context of its developmental and regulatory role vis-à-vis financial markets. The Committee has met three times since the announcement of the Annual Policy Statement in April 2007.

During the second quarter of 2007-08, international financial markets turned volatile as uncertainties about the size and distribution of losses from the US sub-prime mortgage market made investors to adjust their positions. Emerging market economies have generally been less affected by developments in the advanced economies.

Indian financial markets remained orderly for the most part of the second quarter of 2007-08.

The call money rate, which had remained below the reverse repo rate during June-July 2007 on the back of the easing of liquidity conditions and ceiling on absorption through reverse repo operations under the liquidity adjustment facility (LAF) till August 3, 2007, reverted to the corridor set by the reverse repo and repo rates in August-September 2007. Interest rates in the collateralised segment of the overnight money market also hardened but remained below the call rate during the quarter.

In the foreign exchange market, the Indian rupee generally appreciated vis-a-vis all major currencies (US dollar, Euro, Pound sterling and Japanese yen) during the quarter.

Yields in the Government securities market softened.

Banks' deposit and lending rates softened during the second quarter particularly at the upper end of the range of various maturities.

Government Securities Market

The Reserve Bank has endeavoured to broaden and deepen the Government securities market in terms of participants, instruments and processes. Consequent upon the implementation of the Fiscal Responsibility and Budget Management (FRBM) Act, 2003 and withdrawal of the Reserve Bank from the primary segment, development of the Government securities market has assumed vital importance.

(a) State Government Borrowings

(i) Market Borrowings of States: Information Dissemination : In consultation with State Governments, the information on gross allocation inclusive of net allocation, additional allocation and repayments during 2007-08 and the amount that could be raised during the remaining period of 2007-08 as market borrowings by State Governments was disseminated through a press release in September 2007.

(ii) Non-Competitive Bidding Scheme in the Auctions of State Development Loans: To be Operationalised : The Annual Policy Statement of April 2007 proposed to introduce a 'Non-Competitive Bidding Scheme' in the auctions of State Development Loans (SDLs) in the financial year 2007-08 following discussions with State Governments. Accordingly, a scheme for Non-Competitive Bidding Facility was incorporated in the Revised General Notification issued by all State Governments on July 20, 2007. The scheme would be operationalised by March 31, 2008.

(iii) Reissuance of State Government Securities : Reissuance of SDLs has been favoured with a view to building up a critical mass of stock in the gilt market thereby improving the secondary liquidity of such securities. The Reserve Bank, in consultation with State Governments, has proposed to introduce a system of reissuances. Responses received from State Governments in this regard are being examined and it is proposed to re-issue SDLs in the second half of 2007-08.

(iv) Power Bonds : Under the scheme for one-time settlement of outstanding dues of the State Electricity Boards (SEBs) to Central Public Sector Undertakings (CPSUs), power bonds for an aggregate amount of Rs.31,581 crore were issued by 27 State Governments. The repayment of these power bonds started from the year 2006-07. State Governments could exercise the call option for full or part prepayment of their outstanding power bonds on April 1, 2008 as per the terms and conditions of the respective Notifications.

(b) Central Government Securities

FOREIGN EXCHANGE MARKET

The Reserve Bank has taken several initiatives to rationalise and simplify the procedures in the conduct of foreign exchange transactions with a view to facilitating prompt and efficient customer service. Keeping in view the recommendations of the Committee on Fuller Capital Account Convertibility (CFCAC), a number of measures were taken towards liberalisation of foreign exchange transactions.

The pace of implementation of the recommendations of CFCAC was accelerated with regard to foreign exchange outflows. These measures include:

(i) permitting Indian companies as well as registered partnership firms to invest in overseas joint ventures (JV)/wholly owned subsidiaries (WOS) up to 400 per cent of the their net worth under the automatic route;

(ii) increasing the existing limit of 35 per cent of the net worth for portfolio investments by listed companies to 50 per cent of the net worth and dispensing with the requirement of 10 per cent reciprocal share holding in the listed Indian companies by overseas companies;

(iii) increasing the existing limit for prepayment of external commercial borrowings (ECBs) without the Reserve Bank's approval from US $ 400 million to US $ 500 million, subject to compliance with the minimum average maturity period;

(iv) increasing the aggregate ceiling for overseas investments by mutual funds registered with the SEBI from US $ 4 billion to US $ 5 billion while continuing with the existing facility of investing up to US $ 1 billion in overseas Exchange Traded Funds that may be permitted by the SEBI; and

(v) enhancing the existing limit under the Liberalised Remittance Scheme (LRS) for resident individuals from US $ 100,000 to US $ 200,000 per financial year.

In the context of recent global and domestic developments and with a view to giving an opportunity to small and medium enterprises to manage the challenges in global markets, the Reserve Bank, in consultation with the Government of India, permitted all exporters as a temporary measure, to earn interest on their Exchange Earners' Foreign Currency (EEFC) accounts to the extent of outstanding balances of US $ 1 million per exporter. This facility would be valid up to October 31, 2008 and banks are free to determine the rate of interest.

In addition, the coverage of the interest subvention scheme in respect of rupee export credit to specified categories of exporters was widened and the validity of the scheme was extended by three months from December 31, 2007 to March 31, 2008.

(a) Expansion of Hedging Facilities

The range of hedging tools available to the market participants has been further expanded keeping in view the evolution of foreign exchange market.

FACILITY FOR EXPORTERS AND IMPORTERS

Under extant guidelines, exporters and importers are permitted to hedge on the basis of declaration of an exposure and based on past performance criteria as specified.

Market participants have represented to the Reserve Bank that the facility of hedging under the past performance route may be available on a continuous basis. In order to facilitate exporters and importers to hedge their exposures on a dynamic basis, it is now proposed:

to permit reinstatement of the eligible limits under the past performance route to the extent that supporting underlying documents are produced during the term of the hedge undertaken; and

the reinstatement facility would not, however, be available for contracts already cancelled under the scheme.

Oil Refining and Marketing Companies

With a view to facilitating hedging of foreign exchange exposure in respect of oil companies, it is proposed:

to permit oil companies to hedge their foreign exchange exposures to the extent of 50 per cent of their inventory volume as at the end of the previous quarter by using overseas over-the-counter (OTC)/exchange traded derivatives up to a maximum of one year forward.

(b) Currency Futures

The Annual Policy Statement of April 2007 proposed to set up a Working Group on Currency Futures to study the international experience and suggest a suitable framework to operationalise the proposal within the existing legal and regulatory framework. Accordingly, an Internal Working Group on Currency Futures (Chairman: Shri Salim Gangadharan) was set up which studied, inter alia, the experiences of some emerging market economies where currency futures exchanges have been functioning within an environment of capital controls. The Group considered the views of a wide cross section of stakeholders, including banks, industry associations, domestic and international exchanges, and has had extensive and detailed consultations with market participants in the TAC on Money, Foreign Exchange and Government Securities Markets. The Group has explored various options for the proposed currency futures exchange, particularly on aspects like participation, clearing and settlement, market intermediaries, margins, contract design and surveillance mechanism. The draft report of the Group would be placed on the Reserve Bank's website for comments by November 15, 2007.

(c) Derivatives

The Reserve Bank had constituted an Internal Group for preparing consolidated guidelines on derivatives. Based on the recommendations of the Group in respect of foreign exchange derivatives, the following measures are proposed with a view to providing greater flexibility to the residents:

(i) Writing of Options : Currently, corporates are allowed only to purchase options on a stand-alone basis. In certain cases, corporates are permitted to write options as part of a zero cost structure. It is now proposed: to allow importers and exporters having foreign currency exposures to write covered call and put options in both foreign currency/rupee and cross currency and receive premia.

(ii) Running Options Book : In terms of extant guidelines, authorised dealers (ADs) desirous of running options books in foreign currency rupee options are permitted to do so, subject to approval by the Reserve Bank. In order to enable the ADs to manage their risks efficiently, it is proposed: to permit ADs to run cross currency options books, subject to the Reserve Bank's approval.

(iii) Types of Options : Under extant guidelines on foreign currency rupee options, ADs are permitted to offer only plain vanilla European options. In keeping with the gradual evolution of the foreign exchange market and based on market demand, it is now proposed: to permit ADs to offer American options as well.

Floating Rate Bonds

With a view to simplifying the methodology for pricing of floating rate bonds (FRBs) in the secondary market, the Annual Policy Statement of April 2007 had proposed to examine the change in valuation methodology in consultation with Fixed Income Money Market and Derivatives Association (FIMMDA)/Primary Dealers' Association of India (PDAI). Accordingly, a new issuance structure for FRBs has been approved by the TAC on Money, Foreign Exchange and Government Securities Markets and the facility to handle the new issuance structure is being built into the new Negotiated Dealing System (NDS) auction system being developed by the Clearing Corporation of India Limited (CCIL). This is expected to be completed by March 31, 2008.

(c) Development of Market Infrastructure

(i) Repos in the Corporate Bond Market : The High Level Expert Committee on Corporate Bonds and Securitisation (Chairman: Dr. R.H. Patil) had recommended, inter alia, the establishment of a trade reporting platform for better price discovery. The Securities and Exchange Board of India (SEBI) has since operationalised the reporting platforms managed by the two exchanges, namely, the Bombay Stock Exchange (BSE) and the National Stock Exchange (NSE), as well as the industry body, the FIMMDA. As the corporate debt markets develop and the Reserve Bank is assured of availability of fair prices, and an efficient and safe settlement system based on delivery versus payment (DvP) III and Straight Through Processing (STP) is in place, the Reserve Bank is committed to permitting market repos in corporate bonds.

(ii) Reporting Platform for Interest Rate Swaps : In the Annual Policy Statement of April 2007, it was announced that the CCIL would develop a trade reporting platform for Rupee Interest Rate Swaps (IRS). The platform has since been operationalised on August 30, 2007 and banks and Primary Dealers (PDs) have started reporting the IRS and Forward Rate Agreements (FRAs) trades on the platform on a daily basis.

(iii) Interest Rate Derivatives : Interest rate futures were introduced in India in June 2003. In the context of continued financial market developments, the Annual Policy Statement of April 2007 had proposed to set up a Working Group under the aegis of the TAC on Money, Foreign Exchange and Government Securities Markets to study and suggest measures to facilitate the development of the interest rate futures market. Accordingly, the Reserve Bank has constituted a

Working Group on Interest Rate Futures (Chairman: Shri V.K. Sharma) which would review the experience gained so far with interest rate futures with particular reference to product design issues and make recommendations for activating the instrument. The Group would also revisit the recommendations of the earlier Committees in this area and examine regulatory requirements as well as the scope and extent of participation of non-residents while making its own recommendations. The report would be placed on the Reserve Bank's website within three months (by December 31, 2007) after further discussions with the TAC on Money, Foreign Exchange and Government Securities Markets.

(iv) Market Stabilisation Scheme:Revision of Ceiling : A Memorandum of Understanding (MoU) was signed between the Government of India and the Reserve Bank on March 25, 2004 detailing the rationale and operational modalities of the MSS.

The Government of India, in consultation with the Reserve Bank, has periodically raised the ceiling on the outstanding obligations of the Government of India by way of issuance of bills/securities under the MSS for the year 2007-08 to the level of Rs.2,00,000 crore as on October 4, 2007. The Reserve Bank announces the auctions under the MSS, if any, for the succeeding week every Friday.

(v) Guidelines on 'Short Sales' and 'When Issued' Transactions : Currently, 'Short sale' and 'When Issued' transactions are undertaken on the Negotiated Dealing System - Order Matching (NDS-OM) system only. In order to provide further flexibility to participants, it is proposed: to permit covering of 'Short-sale' and 'When Issued' transactions outside the NDS-OM system.

Guidelines in this regard would be issued in consultation with the FIMMDA and the PDAI.

(vi) CSGL Option on NDS-OM : The screen-based order driven anonymous NDS-OM module was operationalised in August 2005 for trading in Government securities. Access to the module was initially extended to banks and PDs and later to other NDS members including insurance companies, mutual funds and bigger provident funds for their proprietary deals. Constituent trading on the NDS-OM was enabled from May 2007 and access to the system was extended to certain 'qualified entities', including deposit taking non-banking financial companies (NBFCs) maintaining gilt accounts with NDS members. It is now proposed: to include systemically important non-deposit taking NBFCs (NBFC-ND-SI) as 'qualified entities' for accessing the NDS-OM using the CSGL route.

CREDIT DELIVERY AND BANKING SERVICES

It has been the endeavour of the Reserve Bank to address the developmental needs of sectors of the economy that are disadvantaged in the credit market, especially agriculture and SMEs, by improving credit delivery mechanisms and making available basic banking services to the widest sections of the society without procedural hassles.

Initiatives taken in this regard include refocus on employment-intensive sectors under priority sector lending; simplification of the procedures for obtaining agricultural loans; reduction of risk weight on loans extended against gold and silver; augmenting credit flow to distressed farmers; revival of the cooperative structure and regional rural banks (RRBs); development of new avenues of credit dispensation such as micro-finance institutions; and legislation for regulating money lending, deepening financial inclusion and improving customer services.

DELIVERY OF CREDIT TO AGRICULTURE AND OTHER SEGMENTS OF PRIORITY SECTOR

Domestic scheduled commercial banks, both public and private, are required to formulate special agricultural credit plans (SACP) in order to achieve a distinct improvement in flow of credit to agriculture.

During 2006-07, disbursements to agriculture by public sector banks (PSBs) and private sector banks under SACP aggregated Rs.1,22,443 crore and Rs.25,360 crore (provisional), respectively, as against the target of Rs.1,80,160 crore and Rs.40,656 crore. Since the inception of the kisan credit card (KCC) scheme in 1998, PSBs have issued 27.27 million KCCs covering an amount of Rs.1,00,226 crore. During 2007-08 (up to June 30), PSBs have issued 0.66 million KCCs covering limits aggregating Rs.5,514 crore (provisional).

The Union Budget, 2007-08 has announced establishment of the Rural Infrastructure Development Fund (RIDF) XIII with the National Bank for Agriculture and Rural Development (NABARD) with a corpus of Rs.12,000 crore and a separate window under the RIDF XIII for rural roads under the Bharat Nirman Programme with a corpus of Rs.4,000 crore. Since the inception of the RIDF, the total allocation under the RIDF (I to XII) was of the order of Rs.64,000 crore.

While cumulative sanctions to State Governments and the National Rural Roads Development Agency (NRRDA) under various tranches of the RIDF (I to XII) stood at Rs.61,312 crore and Rs.4,000 crore, respectively, the cumulative disbursements stood at Rs.38,934 crore (as on July 31, 2007). The disbursements under various tranches of RIDF during 2007-08 (up to July 31) amounted to Rs.1,374 crore.

During 2006-07, various State Governments were sanctioned loans aggregating Rs.10,555 crore, including Rs.1,023 crore sanctioned to the distressed districts of four States viz., Andhra Pradesh, Kerala, Karnataka and Maharashtra.

Priority Sector Lending: Revised Guidelines

Guidelines on lending to the priority sector were revised with effect from April 30, 2007 based on the Technical Paper of the Internal Working Group (Chairman: Shri C. S. Murthy) and the feedback received thereon from the Government of India, banks, financial institutions, NBFCs, associations of industries, media, public and the Indian Banks' Association (IBA).

The revised guidelines focus on ensuring adequate flow of bank credit to weaker segments of the population and to employment-intensive sectors of the economy. The broad categories that are covered under the priority sector include agriculture, small enterprises, retail trade, micro credit, education and housing, subject to certain limits. The revised guidelines also take into account the revised definition of small and micro enterprises envisaged in the Micro, Small and Medium Enterprises Development Act, 2006.

Simplification of the Procedures and Processes for Agricultural Loans

The Working Group (Chairman: Shri C.P. Swarnkar) constituted by the Reserve Bank to examine the documentation, procedures and other requirements prescribed by banks in providing agricultural loans, submitted its report in April 2007 which was placed on the Reserve Bank's website.

On the basis of its recommendations, all SCBs (including RRBs) were advised to dispense with the requirement of submitting 'Nil Dues' Certificate (NDC) for small loans up to Rs.50,000 to small and marginal farmers, share-croppers and the like and, instead, obtain self-declaration from the borrower. Furthermore, in order to overcome the problem of producing identification/status documents, banks were advised to accept certificates provided by local administration/panchayati raj institutions regarding the cultivation of crops in case of loans to landless labourers, share-croppers and oral lessees.

Agricultural Indebtedness: Constitution of Internal Working Group

The Committee on Agricultural Indebtedness (Chairman: Dr. R. Radhakrishna) constituted by the Government of India has submitted its report, which, inter alia, addresses issues relating to creation of credit absorption capacities, need for risk mitigation practices, introduction of cyclical credit system, dispute resolution mechanisms and setting up of a debt redemption fund. It is proposed to constitute an Internal Working Group to examine the Committee's recommendations that are relevant to the banking system in general and the Reserve Bank, in particular. The Group is expected to have consultations with stakeholders and submit its report before December 31, 2007. The Working Group's report will be placed in the public domain for feedback and further processing.

Revival of Rural Co-operative Credit Structure: Status

Based on the recommendations of the Task Force on Revival of Rural Co-operative Credit Institutions (Chairman: Prof.A.Vaidyanathan) and in consultation with State Governments, the Government of India had approved a package for revival of the short-term rural cooperative credit structure. Thirteen States have executed Memoranda of Understanding (MoUs) with the Government of India and the NABARD as envisaged under the package. Implementation and monitoring of the revival package are being overseen by the National Implementing and Monitoring Committee (NIMC) set up by the Government of India. Furthermore, a study on the long-term cooperative credit structure was entrusted to the Task Force by the Government of India which submitted its report in August 2006. The Government is in the process of formulating a package of measures in consultation with State Governments.

Regional Rural Banks: Status and Further Action

The Government of India initiated the process of State-level sponsor bank-wise amalgamation of RRBs in September

2005 in order to strengthen them. Consequent upon amalgamation of 147 RRBs into 46 new RRBs sponsored by 18 banks in 17 States, the total number of RRBs was reduced from 196 to 95.

In order to prepare RRBs to adopt appropriate technology and migrate to core banking solutions for better customer services, it is proposed:

to constitute a Working Group with representatives from the Reserve Bank, the NABARD, sponsor banks and RRBs for preparing a road-map for migration to core banking solutions by RRBs.

The Internal Working Group on RRBs (Chairman: Shri A.V.Sardesai) had recommended that RRBs may be advised to maintain a minimum level of capital to risk-weighted assets ratio (CRAR) which would be progressively raised to the current level of CRAR as per the Basel I norms. At present, capital adequacy norms are not prescribed for RRBs and state/central cooperative banks. In order to further strengthen the capital structure of RRBs and state/central cooperative banks as also in the context of financial stability of the whole system, it is proposed that:

RRBs and state/central cooperative banks should disclose the level of CRAR as on March 31, 2008 in their balance sheets.

a road-map may be evolved for achieving the desired level of CRAR by these banks.

Relief Measures for Distressed Farmers

The Working Group (Chairman: Prof.S.S.Johl) constituted by the Reserve Bank to suggest measures for assisting distressed farmers, including provision of financial counselling services and introduction of a specific Credit Guarantee Scheme under the Deposit Insurance and Credit Guaranee Corporation (DICGC) Act for such farmers, submitted its final report in

November 2006. Based on the recommendations of the Working Group, an Agricultural Loans (Distressed Farmers) Guarantee Scheme, 2007 has been drafted and forwarded to the Government of India. The Scheme is being revised based on the Government's comments.

Technical Group for Review of Legislations on Money Lending

The Technical Group (Chairman: Shri S.C.Gupta) set up to review the efficacy of the existing legislative framework governing money lending and its enforcement machinery in different States and make recommendations to State Governments for improving the legal and enforcement framework in the interest of rural households, submitted its report in July 2007. The report has been forwarded to State Governments for consideration.

Credit Flow to Micro, Small and Medium Enterprises Sector

Consequent upon announcement made in the Annual Policy Statement of April 2007, all State Level Bankers' Committee (SLBC) convenor banks were advised on May 8, 2007 to review their institutional arrangements for delivering credit to the small and medium enterprises (SME) sector, especially in 388 clusters identified by the United Nations Industrial Development Organisation (UNIDO) spread over 21 states in various parts of the country.

Promotion of Livelihood in the Unorganised Sector: Role of Financial System

The National Commission for Enterprises in the Unorganised Sector, under the Chairmanship of Dr. Arjun K.Sengupta has submitted to the Central Government a comprehensive report on 'Conditions of Work and Promotion of Livelihood in the Unorganised Sector'. The report has suggested a package of measures for addressing some critical issues relating to farm and non-farm sectors. Some of the recommendations contained in the report relate to the Indian financial system. In order to study these recommendations and suggest the way forward, it is proposed:

> *to constitute a Working Group to study the various recommendations of the report of the Sengupta Committee which are relevant to the financial system and to suggest an appropriate action plan for implementation of acceptable recommendations. The Group would submit its report within a month.*

Rehabilitation/Nursing of Potentially Viable Sick SME Units

The Standing Advisory Committee on Flow of Institutional Credit to the SME Sector observed in its eighth meeting held on January 16, 2007 that there has been considerable delay in rehabilitation/nursing of the potentially viable sick SME units due to the inability of promoters to bring in additional contribution for rehabilitation/nursing of the units.

As suggested in the meeting, a Working Group has been constituted (Chairman: Dr.K.C. Chakrabarty) with representatives from banks and the Small Industries Development Bank of India (SIDBI) to examine the feasibility of bringing in additional capital through alternative routes such as equity participation and venture financing and suggest remedial measures for those potentially viable sick units which can be rehabilitated at the earliest. The Group is expected to submit its report by December 2007.

Financial Inclusion

(i) Pilot Project for SLBCs for 100 per cent Financial Inclusion: Status and Further Action : So far, 160 districts have been identified for financial inclusion and 100 per cent financial inclusion has been achieved in the Union Territory of Puducherry and in 28 districts in eight States (Andhra Pradesh, Gujarat, Haryana, Himachal Pradesh, Karnataka, Kerala, Punjab and West Bengal).

Notably, all districts of Himachal Pradesh have achieved financial inclusion. An evaluation of the progress made in achieving financial inclusion in these districts is being undertaken to draw lessons for further action in this regard.

(ii) Working Group on Improvement of Banking Services in Lakshadweep: Status : A Working Group (Chairman: Regional Director for Kerala and the Union Territory of Lakshadweep) with members from the Government of the Union Territory, the zonal heads of the NABARD, the SIDBI and the SLBC convenor bank has been constituted to undertake a study of banking services provided in the Union Territory of Lakshadweep. The Group is currently examining the various issues relating to improvement in banking services in the Union Territory.

(iii) Working Group on Improvement of Banking Services in Himachal Pradesh : A Working Group (Chairman: Regional Director for Punjab and Himachal Pradesh and the Union Territory of Chandigarh) has been constituted to review the role of banks and financial institutions in supporting initiatives taken by the State Government of Himachal Pradesh for promoting economic development and recommending measures for enhancing greater outreach/penetration of the banking system in the State. The Group has representatives from the State Government of Himachal Pradesh, the NABARD, the SIDBI and the SLBC convenor bank. The Group submitted its report in September 2007 which is under examination.

(iv) Working Group on Improvement of Banking Services in Jharkhand : With a view to improving banking facilities in certain less developed States/regions, the Reserve Bank had earlier constituted State-specific working groups to suggest necessary developmental initiatives. In pursuance of this policy, a working group for the State of Jharkhand has since been constituted to recommend measures to enhance the outreach of banking services in the State.

(v) Services to Depositors and Small Borrowers in Rural and Semi-Urban Areas: Status : As indicated in the Annual Policy Statement of April 2005, the National Council of Applied Economic Research (NCAER) was entrusted to carry out a study on the quality of services rendered by branches of commercial banks to their customers (both depositors and small borrowers) in the rural and semi-urban areas. The NCAER has since submitted its report which is being placed in the public domain.

(vi) Lead Bank Scheme : The Lead Bank Scheme, introduced in 1969, aimed at coordinating the activities of banks and other development agencies for achieving the overall objectives of enhancing the flow of bank finance to the priority sector and promoting banks' role in overall development of the rural sector. With a focus on financial inclusion and recent developments in the banking sector, and in order to improve the Scheme's effectiveness, it is proposed: to constitute a High Level Committee to review the Lead Bank Scheme.

(vii) Credit Counselling: Setting up of Financial Literacy-cum-Counselling Centres : In the light of the recommendations of the Working Group (Chairman: Prof. S. S. Johl) constituted for suggesting measures for assisting distressed farmers as also the Working Group (Chairman: Shri C. P. Swarnkar) constituted to examine procedures and processes for agricultural loans, SLBC convenor banks were advised to set up a financial literacy-cum-counselling centre in any one district on a pilot basis and extend it to all other districts in due course, based on the experience gained. Several banks have since taken initiatives in opening credit counselling centres in the country. In order to take this initiative forward it is proposed: to prepare a concept paper on the subject detailing the future course of action and place it on the Reserve Bank's website for feedback.

(viii) Information and Communication Technology to Enhance Financial Inclusion : Widespread use of Information and Communication Technology (ICT) is expected to make 100 per cent financial inclusion a feasible goal in terms of convenience, delivery, cost effectiveness, reliability and security for costumers as well as providers of financial services. The initial cost in rolling out such technology-based services could hinder the path of financial inclusion. Furthermore, in certain remote areas, the unavailability of electricity supply may also require investment in solar power generating devices for use of ICT. It is, therefore, proposed: to provide financial assistance to RRBs for defraying a part of their initial cost in implementing ICT-based solutions, including installation of solar power generating devices for powering ICT equipment in remote and under-served areas.

Micro-finance

The self help group (SHG)-Bank Linkage Programme has emerged as the major micro-finance programme in the country and is being implemented by commercial banks, RRBs and co-operative banks. By 2006-07, 29,24,973 SHGs were credit-linked to banks, with cumulative bank loans of Rs.18,047 crore.

Customer Service in the Reserve Bank

It has been the endeavour of the Reserve Bank to improve the quality of its public services to the common person and reduce transaction costs as well as time, both for the Reserve Bank and the citizens/organisations.

A Committee on Procedures and Performance Audit on Public Services (CPPAPS) (Chairman: Shri S.S. Tarapore) was set up in 2003 to undertake procedures and performance audit on public services and regulatory clearances in the Reserve Bank and to coordinate with the Committees on Customer Services set up by banks. It has now been proposed to constitute a Committee (Chairman: Shri Prabhakar Rao) to evaluate customer services rendered by the Reserve Bank.

The Committee would evaluate the efforts for improving public services to common persons undertaken by the Reserve Bank since the adoption of the recommendations of the CPPAPS, review the existing policies and procedures and suggest improvement in the quality of services.

INFORMATION TECHNOLOGY SUPPORT TO UCBS

Considerable progress has been made in the area of human resources development for facilitating the growth of the UCB sector, pursuant to the Reserve Bank entering into MoUs with State Governments and the Government of India.

During 2006-08, 69 programmes have been held in which 675 Directors, 515 Executives, 163 Auditors have participated with a view to professionalising the management of UCBs.

In furtherance of commitments under the MoUs and with a view to identifying the areas requiring IT support for UCBs, it is proposed:

> *to constitute a working group comprising representatives of the Reserve Bank, State Governments and the UCB sector to examine the various areas where IT support could be provided by the Reserve Bank.*

COMMITTEE ON FINANCIAL SECTOR ASSESSMENT

The Annual Policy Statement of April 2007 outlined the approach and progress made by the Committee on Financial Sector Assessment (CFSA) (Chairman: Dr.Rakesh Mohan; Co-Chairman: Dr.D.Subbarao) to undertake a self-assessment of the Indian financial sector.

As envisaged, the CFSA has constituted four Advisory Panels for the assessment of Financial Stability and Stress Testing, Financial Regulation and Supervision, Institutions and Market Structure and Transparency Standards. The Advisory Panels would prepare separate reports covering each of the above aspects. These Advisory Panels comprise of non-official experts with domain knowledge in respective areas and officials with similar expertise represented as Special Invitees.

The Advisory Panel on Financial Stability and Stress Testing (Chairman: Shri M.B.N. Rao) would conduct macro-prudential surveillance (including system-level stress testing) to assess the soundness and stability of financial system and suggest measures for strengthening the financial structure and system and its development in a medium-term perspective.

The other three Advisory Panels would identify and consider the relevant standards and codes as currently prescribed and applicable to different areas, evaluate their implementation in the Indian context, identify gaps in adherence to respective standards and suggest possible roadmaps towards compliance in a medium-term perspective.

The Advisory Panel on Financial Regulation and Supervision (Chairman: Shri M.S. Verma) would consider the relevant standards and codes applicable for financial regulation and supervision pertaining to the banking sector, financial markets and insurance; the Advisory Panel on Institutions and Market Structure (Chairman: Shri C.M. Vasudev) would consider the relevant standards and codes applicable to bankruptcy laws, accounting and auditing, payment and settlement systems and corporate governance policies; and the Advisory Panel on Transparency Standards (Chairman: Shri Nitin Desai) would consider the relevant standards and codes applicable for transparency in monetary, financial, fiscal and data dissemination policies.

The CFSA, before setting up of the Advisory Panels, had set up Technical Groups comprising of officials representing mainly regulatory agencies and the Government in all the above-mentioned subject areas which have progressed with technical work in their respective areas. These Groups also provide the Advisory Panels with technical notes and background material as necessary.

The CFSA submitted an interim report delineating its approach and reviewing the progress of work to the Finance Minister and Governor, Reserve Bank of India in July 2007. As mentioned in the Annual Policy Statement, the CFSA would publish Advisory Panel reports and also its own Synthesis Report. Based on an objective analysis of the present strengths and weaknesses of the financial sector and the status with regard to standards, the CFSA is also expected to lay out a road-map for further reforms in a medium-term perspective. The CFSA is expected to complete the assessment by March 2008.

PRUDENTIAL MEASURES

The Reserve Bank has been adapting regulatory and supervisory tools to facilitate appropriate evolution of the financial system. The endeavour has been to anchor public confidence, to engage in financial development to support accelerated economic growth and to adopt international best practices with regard to prudential regulations, disclosure standards and supervisory processes.

Discussion Paper on Holding Companies in Banking Groups

In many countries, deregulation and financial consolidation has led to the development of financial holding companies (commercial banking, insurance, investment banking and other financial activities are conducted under the same corporate umbrella). Different financial services within the same organisation are purveyed using different conglomerate models, viz., the universal bank, the bank subsidiary and the bank holding company. These conglomerate models can have one or more layers of intermediate holding companies. Accordingly, a discussion paper on holding companies in banking groups has been placed on the Reserve Bank's website for feedback. Guidelines in this regard would be issued by end-November 2007.

Guidelines on Asset-Liability Management System: Amendments

The Reserve Bank had issued guidelines on the Asset-Liability Management (ALM) system in February 1999, which covered, inter alia, interest rate risk and liquidity risk measurement/reporting framework and prudential limits. Having regard to the international practices, the level of sophistication of banks in India and the need for a sharper assessment of the efficacy of liquidity management, these guidelines have been reviewed and amended with reference to the approach to the measurement of liquidity risk, mismatches and the structural liquidity as also the frequency of supervisory reporting. Operational guidelines in this regard have since been issued.

Introduction of Credit Default Swaps

The recent amendments to the Reserve Bank of India Act, 1934 has provided legality of OTC derivative instruments, including credit derivatives, and accordingly the Annual Policy Statement of April 2007 proposed to permit banks and PDs to begin transacting in single-entity credit default swaps (CDS). The draft guidelines on CDS were placed on the Reserve Bank's website for wider dissemination and comments. On the basis of the feedback, revised draft guidelines have been placed on the Reserve Bank's website for a second round of consultation and final guidelines would be issued by end-November 2007.

Bank Finance to Factoring Companies: Review of Existing Guidelines

In view of difficulties expressed by some banks, a Working Group has been constituted with representatives from banks, factoring companies and the Reserve Bank to review the existing guidelines regarding financing of factoring companies. The Group would submit its report by November 15, 2007.

Differentiated Bank Licences

The Annual Policy Statement of April 2007 proposed to prepare a technical paper on differentiated bank licences with a view to directing the resources of banks to their niche areas and to sustain efficiency in the banking system which can be equally applicable to both domestic and foreign banks. The technical paper has been placed on the Reserve Bank's website on October 19, 2007.

The paper examined the statutory background of licensing of banks, the existing policies of licensing of private sector banks and foreign banks, international experiences and practices, and pros and cons of the introduction of a differentiated bank licensing regime. The paper recommended that in order to enable the banking system to operate at optimum efficiency and in the interest of financial inclusion, it would be necessary for all banks to offer certain minimum services to all customers, while allowing sufficient freedom to function according to their own business models. The paper also recommended continuation of the existing system for the time being.

Recovery Agents Engaged by Banks

In view of the rise in the number of litigations against banks for engaging recovery agents in the recent past, it is felt that the adverse publicity could result in serious reputational risk for the banking sector as a whole. An urgent need has, therefore, arisen to review the policy, practice, procedure involved in the engagement of recovery agents by banks in India. Accordingly, banks are urged to follow prescribed specific considerations while engaging recovery agents.

Complaints received by the Reserve Bank regarding abusive practices followed by a bank's recovery agents would invite serious supervisory disapproval. The Reserve Bank would consider imposing a temporary ban (or even a permanent ban in case of persistent abusive practices) for engaging recovery agents on those banks where strictures have been passed/ penalties have been imposed by a High Court/Supreme Court or against its Directors/Officers with regard to the abusive practices followed by their recovery agents. An operational circular in this regard would be issued by November 15, 2007.

Cross-border Supervision

Cross-border supervision has assumed importance in view of rapid integration of financial markets as also the heightened pace of merger and acquisition activities worldwide. In this context, the present system of informal exchange of information and supervisory cooperation amongst regulators need to be enhanced and well structured, particularly for internationally active banks. Accordingly, it is proposed: to constitute a working group to lay down the road-map for adoption of a suitable framework for cross-border supervision and supervisory cooperation with overseas regulators, consistent with the framework envisaged in the Basel Committee on Banking Supervision (BCBS).

Consolidated Supervision and Financial Conglomerate Monitoring Mechanism: Integration

Guidelines for consolidated accounting and other quantitative methods to facilitate consolidated supervision were issued to banks in February 2003, based on recommendations of the report of a multi-disciplinary working group (Chairman: Shri Vipin Malik).

Consolidated supervision is undertaken through consolidated financial statements (CFSs) which are intended for public disclosure, consolidated prudential reports (CPRs) for supervisory assessment of risks that could be transmitted to banks by other group members, and compliance with prudential norms on group basis.

The financial conglomerates (FC) monitoring framework was put in place on the basis of the recommendations of the report of the Inter-regulatory Working Group (Chairperson: Smt. Shyamala Gopinath) on monitoring of Systemically Important Financial Intermediaries (Financial Conglomerates).

The focus of the FC return is mainly on intra-group transactions and exposures (both fund-based and non-fund based transactions). The dominant/major entity in the group, called a 'designated entity' (DE), collects and collates FC data/ information and forwards them to the principal regulator for analysis.

The evaluation of overall risks and possible transfer thereof within the group structure, however, needs to be evolved under the consolidated supervision process for bank-led conglomerates.

Accordingly, in order to enhance the effectiveness of the banking supervisory system for bank-led conglomerates, it is proposed to integrate the process of consolidated supervision with the financial conglomerate monitoring mechanism. Draft guidelines in this regard would be placed on the Reserve Bank's website by end-January 2008.

Monitoring Banks' Exposure to Derivatives

At present, supervision of derivatives transactions by banks is carried out through on-site inspection during the annual financial inspection of banks and off-site monitoring of exposures through specified returns.

In view of the potential of derivatives instruments to amplify systemic risks, there is a need to put in place a comprehensive oversight structure targeting the credit risk and operational risk in addition to the market risk, as at present. Furthermore, supervisory oversight needs to include stress testing of derivatives portfolios of banks for credit risk, particularly in view of banks resorting to multi-lateral netting for their counter party exposures. In view of majority of derivatives being over the counter (OTC) products, it is proposed:

> *to cover, besides general market risk, specific risk, especially the credit risk arising out of deficient documentation or settlement risk, under the supervisory process.*

Implementation of Basel II - Pillar 2

The Reserve Bank issued final guidelines on implementation of Basel II framework in regard to Pillar 1 and Pillar 3 in April 2007.

As regards Pillar 2, banks were advised to put in place internal capital adequacy assessment process (ICAAP) to capture all material risks, including those that are partly covered or not covered under the other two Pillars, with the approval of their boards.

The ICAAP of banks are required to be subject to a supervisory review evaluation process (SREP) for which the structure and methodologies for identification and quantification of various risks (not covered under Pillar 1) and provision of additional capital or controls/management actions are being worked out.

Supervisory Review Process

The Mid-term Review of October 2005 had indicated the initiation of a supervisory review process (SRP) for select banks having significant exposure to some sectors, namely, real estate, highly leveraged NBFCs, venture capital funds and capital markets, in order to ensure that effective risk mitigants and sound internal control systems are in place.

In the first round of SRP, a framework was developed for monitoring the systemically important individual banks. The second round of SRP analysed the exposure to sensitive sectors, in particular, to the real estate and capital market sectors of select banks.

Ten banks were identified as outliers based on the real estate and capital market exposures in excess of 200 per cent and 25 per cent, respectively, of their net worth.

The initial analysis revealed that prima facie, all banks under review had put in place risk management policies and systems and controls to manage risks arising from exposures to sensitive sectors.

In case of exposures to real estate, certain irregularities were observed with regard to the implementation of banks' own approved policies. Accordingly, banks were advised to improve risk management processes at operating levels. Furthermore, banks were provided with an indicative list of deficiencies and irregularities and were advised to explicitly spell out the required norms for lending to the real estate sector in their policies.

INSTITUTIONAL DEVELOPMENTS : PAYMENT SYSTEMS

The Reserve Bank continued to strengthen the framework for payment and settlement systems by utilising the full potential of information technology (IT) to improve operational efficiency. The main focus has been on ensuring business continuity, prompt customer service and development of electronic payment products.

Eligibility Criteria for Access to Payment Systems

An Internal Working Group, constituted to prepare comprehensive draft guidelines on minimum eligibility criteria for direct members of the clearing houses, submitted its report in September 2007 which has been placed on the Reserve Bank's website for public comments.

The Group has recommended a set of financial parameters as criteria for clearing house membership and has also suggested for periodical review of compliance by members with a view to ensuring continued safety and soundness of the system.

Annual Review of Payment and Settlement Systems

188. The Annual Policy Statement of April 2007 proposed an annual review of payment and settlement systems and accordingly, its first review was undertaken for the year ended March 31, 2007. The comments/views of banks, chambers of commerce and industry/trade bodies were obtained on the review and a policy paper would be placed on the Reserve Bank's website by November 15, 2007.

Adequacy of Business Continuity Plans

The Annual Policy Statement of April 2007 emphasised adequate business continuity plans by banks as part of disaster recovery management, with a view to ensuring continuous and prompt customer services.

With increasing reliance on the use of IT-based processing of day-to-day operations for extending banking and financial services, ensuring appropriate business continuity plans assumes critical importance. The Reserve Bank conducts regular and periodic drills in respect of critical inter-bank systems in order to facilitate banking services and ensure continuity.

The level of preparedness by the participating banks in these exercises conducted by the Reserve Bank is, however, inadequate. Banks are urged to ensure that adequate disaster recovery systems are put in place so as to fully comply with the requirements of the next drill of the Reserve Bank.

Implementation of Core Banking Systems

Implementation of core banking systems (CBS) for banking operations has increased and banks have been encouraged to install the CBS in a phased manner. In view of the advantages of these systems in promoting better costumer services, banks are urged to draw up time-bound action plans for implementation of CBS across all their branches.

Electronic Payment Products: Status and Proposed Action

The coverage of the Real Time Gross Settlement (RTGS) system has increased significantly. By October 23, 2007 RTGS connectivity was available in more than 34,023 branches and the Reserve Bank continues to improve the quality of services through the RTGS. Banks having their branches under the core banking solution can derive maximum benefits out of this system. It is proposed to draw up an action plan for its implementation in consultation with banks. The Committee (Chairman: Dr.R.B. Barman) constituted for introduction of the National Settlement System (NSS) examined various models and recommended the Centralised Funds Transfer System (CFTS) model for implementation. Under the CFTS model, banks would be able to transfer funds across all Deposit Accounts Departments (DADs) on real time basis.

The CFTS interface would enable the member banks to transfer funds from surplus centre for meeting the clearing obligations smoothly. So far, 11 DADs - Mumbai, Chennai, New Delhi, Kolkata, Hyderabad, Bangalore, Nagpur, Ahmedabad, Chandigarh, Kanpur and Jaipur - have been connected to the CFTS. The remaining five centres would be connected after the system stabilises in these 11 centres.

The Electronic Clearing Service (ECS), which facilitates bulk payments, is currently available at 67 centres. The Reserve Bank proposes to operationalise the National Electronic Clearing Service (NECS) using the existing infrastructure of National Electronic Funds Transfer (NEFT) system with a view to widening the geographical coverage of the ECS. Under the NECS, the clearing and settlement would be centralised at Mumbai. Banks would receive their ECS centrally and transfer the transactions either on their core banking solution or arrange to distribute to their branches.

3

Different Systems of Banking

INTRODUCTION

Rural banking in India started since the establishment of banking sector in India. Rural Banks in those days mainly focussed upon the agro sector. Regional rural banks in India penetrated every corner of the country and extended a helping hand in the growth process of the country.

SBI has 30 Regional Rural Banks in India known as RRBs. The rural banks of SBI is spread in 13 states extending from Kashmir to Karnataka and Himachal Pradesh to North East. The total number of SBIs Regional Rural Banks in India branches is 2349 (16%). Till date in rural banking in India, there are 14,475 rural banks in the country of which 2126 (91%) are located in remote rural areas.

Apart from SBI, there are other few banks which functions for the development of the rural areas in India. Few of them are as follows.

COOPERATIVE APEX BANK LIMITED

The Haryana State Cooperative Apex Bank Ltd. commonly called as HARCOBANK plays a vital role in rural banking in the economy of Haryana State and has been providing aids and financing farmers, rural artisans, agricultural labourers, entrepreneurs, etc. in the state and giving service to its depositors.

NABARD

National Bank for Agriculture and Rural Development (NABARD) is a development bank in the sector of Regional Rural Banks in India.

It provides and regulates credit and gives service for the promotion and development of rural sectors mainly agriculture, small scale industries, cottage and village industries, handicrafts. It also finance rural crafts and other allied rural economic activities to promote integrated rural development. It helps in securing rural prosperity and its connected matters.

Sindhanur Urban Souharda Co-operative Bank

Sindhanur Urban Souharda Co-operative Bank, popularly known as SUCO BANK is the first of its kind in rural banks of India. The impressive story of its inception is interesting and inspiring for all the youth of this country.

United Bank of India

United Bank of India (UBI) also plays an important role in regional rural banks. It has expanded its branch network in a big way to actively participate in the developmental of the rural and semi-urban areas in conformity with the objectives of nationalisation.

Syndicate Bank

Syndicate Bank was firmly rooted in rural India as rural banking and have a clear vision of future India by understanding the grassroot realities. Its progress has been abreast of the phase of progressive banking in India especially in rural banks.

FOREIGN BANKS IN INDIA

Foreign Banks in India always brought an explanation about the prompt services to customers. After the set up foreign banks in India, the banking sector in India also become competitive and accurative.

New rules announced by the Reserve Bank of India for the foreign banks in India in this budget has put up great hopes among foreign banks which allows them to grow unfettered. Now foreign banks in India are permitted to set up local subsidiaries.

The policy conveys that forign banks in India may not acquire Indian ones (except for weak banks identified by the RBI, on its terms) and their Indian subsidiaries will not be able to open branches freely. Please see the list of Foreign banks in India till date.

List of Foreign Banks in India

- ABN-AMRO Bank
- Abu Dhabi Commercial Bank
- Bank of Ceylon
- BNP Paribas Bank
- Citi Bank
- China Trust Commercial Bank
- Deutsche Bank
- HSBC
- JPMorgan Chase Bank
- Standard Chartered Bank
- Scotia Bank
- Taib Bank

By the year 2009, the list of foreign banks in India is going to become more quantitative as number of foreign banks are still waiting with baggage to start business in India.

Upcoming Foreign Banks in India

By 2009 few more names is going to be added in the list of foreign banks in India. This is as an aftermath of the sudden interest shown by Reserve Bank of India paving roadmap for foreign banks in India greater freedom in India. Among them is the world's best private bank by EuroMoney magazine, Switzerland's UBS.

The following are the list of foreign banks going to set up business in India

- Royal Bank of Scotland
- Switzerland's UBS
- US-based GE Capital
- Credit Suisse Group
- Industrial and Commercial Bank of China

Merrill Lynch is having a joint venture in Indian investment banking space -- DSP Merrill Lynch. Goldman Sachs holds stakes in Kotak Mahindra arms.

GE Capital is also having a wide presence in consumer finance through GE Capital India.

India's GDP is seen growing at a robust pace of around 7% over the next few years, throwing up opportunities for the banking sector to profit from.

The credit of banks has risen by over 25% in 2004-05 and the growth momentum is expected to continue over the next four to five years.

Participation in the growth curve of the Indian economy in the next four years will provide foreign banks a launch pad for greater business expansion when they get more freedom after April 2009.

BANKING SERVICES IN INDIA

With years, banks are also adding services to their customers. The Indian banking industry is passing through a phase of customers market. The customers have more choices in choosing their banks. A competition has been established within the banks operating in India.

With stiff competition and advancement of technology, the services provided by banks has become more easy and convenient. The past days are witness to an hour wait before withdrawing cash from accounts or a cheque from north of the country being cleared in one month in the south.

This section of banking deals with the latest discovery in the banking instruments along with the polished version of their old systems.

Bank Account

Open bank account - the most common and first service of the banking sector. There are different types of bank account in Indian banking sector. The bank accounts are as follows:

- Bank Savings Account - Bank Savings Account can be opened for eligible person / persons and certain organisations / agencies (as advised by Reserve Bank of India (RBI) from time to time)
- Bank Current Account - Bank Current Account can be opened by individuals / partnership firms / Private and Public Limited Companies / HUFs / Specified Associates / Societies / Trusts, etc.
- Bank Term Deposits Account - Bank Term Deposits Account can be opened by individuals / partnership firms / Private and Public Limited Companies / HUFs/ Specified Associates / Societies / Trusts, etc.
- Bank Account Online - With the advancement of technology, the major banks in the public and private sector has faciliated their customer to open bank account online. Bank account online is registered through a PC with an internet connection. The advent of bank account online has saved both the cost of operation for banks as well as the time taken in opening an account.

Note :- A minor account can be opened but jointly with a

guardian and only the guardian would is allowed to operate the account.

General Procedure to Open an Account

- The Bank will provide you with details of various types of accounts that you may open with the Bank.
- You can have your choice on what type of account would best suit you, based on your needs and requirements
- The Bank will, prior to opening an account, require documentation and information as prescribed by the "Know Your Customer" (KYC) guidelines issued by RBI and or such other norms or procedures adopted by the Bank prior to opening the account.
- The due diligence process that the Bank would follow, will involve providing documentation verifying your identity, verifying your address, and information onyour occupation or business and source of funds. As part of the due diligence process the Bank may also require an introduction from a person acceptable to the Bank if they so deem necessary and will need your recent photographs.
- The Bank is required by law to obtain Permanent Account Number (PAN) or General Index Register (GIR) Number or, where you do not possess such registration, declaration in Form No. 60 or 61 as specified under the Income Tax Rules.
- In the event that the account opening process is likely to take longer than normal, the Bank will inform you of the revised timeline.
- You can also call your branch or the executive for any queries that you may have and the branch / executive will revert on the query at the earliest.

- The Bank will provide you with the account opening forms and other relevant material to enable you open the account. Bank personnel will advise you on the complete details of information that would be required by the Bank for the verification process.
- The Bank reserves the right, at its sole discretion, to open any account and at such terms as the Bank may prescribe from time to time

PLASTIC MONEY

Credit Card

Credit cards in India is gaining ground. A number of banks in India are encouraging people to use credit card. The concept of credit card was used in 1950 with the launch of charge cards in USA by Diners Club and American Express. Credit card however became more popular with use of magnetic strip in 1970.

Credit card in India became popular with the introduction of foreign banks in the country.

Credit cards are financial instruments, which can be used more than once to borrow money or buy products and services on credit. Basically banks, retail stores and other businesses issue these.

Major Banks issuing Credit Card in India

- State Bank of India credit card (SBI credit card)
- Bank of Baroda credit card or BoB credit card
- ICICI credit card
- HDFC credit card
- IDBI credit card
- ABN AMRO credit card

- Standard Chartered credit card
- HSBC credit card
- Citibank Credit Card

Precautions taken After Receiving Credit Card

To Avoid:

- Bending the Card.
- Exposure to electronic devices and gadgets.
- Direct exposure to sunlight.
- Be cautious about disclosing your account number over the phone unless you know you're dealing with a reputable company.
- Never put your account number on the outside of an envelope or on a postcard.
- Draw a line through blank spaces on charge or debit slips above the total so the amount cannot be changed.
- Don't sign a blank charge or debit slip.
- Tear up carbons and save your receipts to check against your monthly statements.
- Cut up old cards - cutting through the account number - before disposing of them.
- Open monthly statements promptly and compare them with your receipts. Report mistakes or discrepancies as soon as possible to the special address listed on your statement for inquiries. Under the FCBA (credit cards) and the EFTA (ATM or debit cards), the card issuer must investigate errors reported to them within 60 days of the date your statement was mailed to you.
- Keep a record - in a safe place separate from your cards - of your account numbers, expiration dates, and the telephone numbers of each card issuer so you can report

a loss quickly.

- Carry only those cards that you anticipate you'll need.

To Do:

- Please sign on the signature panel on the reverse of the Card immediately with a non-erasable ball-point pen (preferably in black ink). This will ensure that the benefits of membership are yours and yours alone.
- Keep the Card in a prominent place in your wallet. You will notice if it is missing.

Resons credit card being rejected at retail outlet:

- One may have exceeded the borrowing limit or defaulted (constantly) on minimum payment due.
- The Card is hotlisted.
- The card has crossed its expiration date.
- Non-receipt of dues of one-card blocks future transactions on any other card(s) held of the same card-issuing bank.
- The magnetic stripe on the reverse of the card is damaged i.e. has been scratched or exposed to continuous heat/direct sunlight or magnetic field-like card kept near a TV set / other electronic appliances.
- Systems or technology failures have in rare instances also led to non acceptance of cards when swiped through an Electronic Terminal.

GLOBAL PLAYER IN CREDIT CARD MARKET

MasterCard

MasterCard is a product of MasterCard International and along with VISA are distributed by financial institutions around the world. Cardholders borrow money against a line of credit and pay it back with interest if the balance is carried over from month to month. Its products are issued by 23,000 financial institutions in 220 countries and territories. In 1998, it had almost 700 million cards in circulation, whose users spent $650 billion in more than 16.2 million locations.

VISA Card

VISA cards is a product of VISA USA and along with MasterCard is distributed by financial institutions around the world. A VISA cardholder borrows money against a credit line and repays the money with interest if the balance is carried over from month to month in a revolving line of credit. Nearly 600 million cards carry one of the VISA brands and more than 14 million locations accept VISA cards.

American Express

The world's favorite card is American Express Credit Card. More than 57 million cards are in circulation and growing and it is still growing further. Around US $ 123 billion was spent last year through American Express Cards and it is poised to be the world's No. 1 card in the near future. In a regressive US economy last year, the total amount spent on American Express cards rose by 4 percent. American Express cards are very popular in the U.S., Canada, Europe and Asia and are used widely in the retail and everyday expenses segment.

Diners Club International

Diners Club is the world's No. 1 Charge Card. Diners Club cardholders reside all over the world and the Diners Card is a alltime favourite for corporates. There are more than 8 million Diners Club cardholders. They are affluent and are frequent travelers in premier businesses and institutions, including Fortune 500 companies and leading global corporations.

JCB Cards

The JCB Card has a merchant network of 10.93 million in approximately 189 countries. It is supported by over 320 financial institutions worldwide and serves more than 48 million cardholders in eighteen countries world wide. The JCB philosophy of "identify the customer's needs and please the customer with Service from the Heart" is paying rich dividends as their customers spend US$43 billion annually on their JCB cards.

Grace / Interest Free Period

The number of days you have on a card before a card issuer starts charging you interest is called grace period. Usually this period is the number of days between the statement date and the due date of payment. Grace periods on credit cards are usually 2-3 weeks. However, there is likely to be no grace for balances carried forward from previous month and fresh purchases thereafter if any.

The following are some of the varieties of credit cards in India

- ANZ - Gold
- ANZ - Silver
- Bank Of India - Indiacard
- Bol - Taj Premium
- Bol - Gold
- BoB - Exclusive
- BoB - Premium
- Canara Bank - Cancard
- Citibank - Gold
- Citibank - Silver
- Citibank WWF Card
- Citibank Visa Card for Women
- Citibank Cry Card
- Citibank Silver International Credit Card

- Citibank Women's International Credit Card
- Citibank Gold International Credit Card
- Citibank Electronic Credit Card
- Citibank Maruti International Credit Card
- Citibank Times Card
- Citibank Indian Oil International Credit Card
- Citibank Citi Diners Club Card
- HSBC - Gold
- HSBC - Classic
- ICICI Sterling Silver Credit Card
- ICICI Solid Gold Credit Card
- ICICI True Blue Credit Card
- SBI Card
- Stanchart - Gold
- Stanchart - Executive
- Stanchart - Classic
- Thomas Cook Standard Chartered Global Credit Card

Standard Segregation of Credit Cards

- Standard Card - It is the most basic card (sans all frills) offered by issuers.
- Classic Card - Brand name for the standard card issued by VISA.
- Gold Card/Executive Card - A credit card that offers a higher line of credit than a standard card. Income eligibility is also higher. In addition, issuers provide extra perks or incentives to cardholders.
- Platinum Card - A credit card with a higher limit and additional perks than a gold card.

- Titanium Card - A card with an even higher limit than a platinum card.

The following are some of the plus features of credit card in India :

- Hotel discounts
- Travel fare discounts
- Free global calling card
- Lost baggage insurance
- Accident insurance
- Insurance on goods purchased
- Waiver of payment in case of accidental death
- Household insurance

Some Facts of Credit Cards

- The first card was issued in India by Visa in 1981.
- The country's first Gold Card was also issued from Visa in 1986.
- The first international credit card was issued to a restricted number of customers by Andhra Bank in 1987 through the Visa program, after getting special permission from the Reserve Bank of India.
- The credit cards are shape and size, as specified by the ISO 7810 standard. It is generally of plastic quality. It is also sometimes known as Plastic Money.

FAQs

What does Grace / Interest Free Period Mean?

The number of days given to you on your card before the card issuer starts charging you interest is called grace period. Generally the grace period is the number of days between the statement date and the due date of payment. Grace periods on credit cards are usually 2-3 weeks. However, there is likely to be no grace for balances carried forward from previous month and fresh purchases thereafter if any.

What is implied in Cash Advance?

Cash advances on Credit Cards are convenient and the easiest facility to utilise. Manority of the banks in India charge a transaction fee as well as service fee / interest charge on cash advances. This service fee accrues from the date of the advance (as soon as you receive the cash) to the date of full payment. The charges varies from banks to banks. Cash advance facility is a part of the overall credit limit assigned to a cardholder. The limit is of cash acvance is always lesser than the borrowing limit or the credit limit.

How to make payments from Dubai to the already existing Citibank cards in India. How to avail of the statements to know the current bank balance of each card. Is online facility available?

According to RBI " Resident Indians may be nominated as additional/add-on card holders by non-residents. However, the non-residents from their foreign currency funds should meet claims arising out of use of such cards by residents only.In cases where the cards have been arranged by NRIs these liabilities may be met out of NRE/FCNR accounts in India also. Under no circumstances will any remittance be allowed by residents from India to settle their claims against use of such additional/add-on cards". NRIs get rupee credit cards which are valid for use in India, Nepal and Bhutan.

Can I use my Global credit card on the net to pay some US company for web hosting charges? or I have to obtain permission from RBI. If any permissions are needed, How to get them?

The RBI's exchange control manual mentions that 'International Credit Cards' can be used for "Registration of Internet domain name, hosting charges for website/home pages overseas and access fees for Internet related services through website". Before using your Global Credit Card on the net for web hosting charges, you further clarify the aforesaid issue or seek permission from your card issuer. Even get in touch with the card issuing bank or organisation directly for such clarifications.

How will I know if my Credit Card application has got approved?

It is suggested to give your mobile number and e-mail id at the time of application for the Credit Card. This will help the issuer to intimate you either through SMS or through e-mail with the approved status of your application. You will also receive a letter by post informing you of the Card approval. You should be receiving your Card around the same time as the approval letter.

How will I know if my Credit Card application has got declined?

You will receive a letter from the Bank even if your application for Card is not approved. If in case there is a further information of missing documents, you will be sent a letter asking for the same. Then you need to fulfil with the documents to the specified address.

What to do if Credit Card is Lost or Stolen?

Report the loss or theft of your credit cards to the card issuers to the earliest through their 24-hour helpline service. Follow up your phone calls with a letter. Include your account number, when you noticed your card was missing, and the date you first reported the loss.

After doing these, check your homeowner's insurance policy to see if it covers your liability for card thefts. If yes its fine otherwise change your policy to include this protection.

Before the intimation, different banks have their own limit of loss bearing by the card holder. After the intimation, it is the bank who bears the loss if any amount is spent.

Debit Card

Debit cards, also known as check cards look like credit cards or ATM cards (automated teller machine card). It operate like cash or a personal check. Debit cards are different from credit cards. Credit card is a way to "pay later," whereas debit card is a way to "pay now." When we use a debit card, our money is quickly deducted from the bank account.

Debit cards are accepted at many locations, including grocery stores, retail stores, gasoline stations, and restaurants. Its an alternative to carrying a checkbook or cash.

With debit card, we use our own money and not the issuer's money.

In India almost all the banks issue debit card to its account holders.

Features of Debit Card

- Obtaining a debit card is often easier than obtaining a credit card.
- Using a debit card instead of writing checks saves you from showing identification or giving out personal information at the time of the transaction.
- Using a debit card frees you from carrying cash or a checkbook.
- Using a debit card means you no longer have to stock up on traveler's checks or cash when you travel.
- Debit cards may be more readily accepted by merchants than checks, especially in other states or countries wherever your card brand is accepted.
- The debit card is a quick, "pay now" product, giving you no grace period.
- Using a debit card may mean you have less protection than with a credit card purchase for items which are

never delivered, are defective, or were misrepresented. But, as with credit cards, you may dispute unauthorized charges or other mistakes within 60 days. You should contact the card issuer if a problem cannot be resolved with the merchant.

- Returning goods or canceling services purchased with a debit card is treated as if the purchase were made with cash or a check.

Tips for Responsible use of Debit Card

- If your card is lost or stolen, report the loss immediately to your financial institution.
- If you suspect your card is being fraudulently used, report it immediately to your financial institution.
- Hold on to your receipts from your debit card transactions.

  A thief may get your name and debit card number from a receipt and order goods by mail or over the telephone. Your card does not have to be missing in order for it to be misused.
- If you have a PIN number, memorize it. Do not keep your PIN number with your card. Also, don't choose a PIN number that a smart thief could figure out, such as your phone number or birthday.
- Never give your PIN number to anyone. Keep your PIN private.
- Always know how much money you have available in your account. Don't forget that your debit card may allow you to access money that you have set aside to cover a check which has not cleared your bank yet.
- Keep your receipts in one place -- for easy retrieval and better oversight of your bank account.

LOANS

Banks in India with the way of development have become easy to apply in loan market. The following loans are given by almost all the banks in the country:

- Personal Loan
- Car Loan or Auto Loan
- Loan against Shares
- Home Loan
- Education Loan or Student Loan

In Personal Loan, one can get a sanctioned loan amount between Rs 25,000 to 10,00,000 depending upon the profile of person applying for the loan. SBI, ICICI, HDFC, HSBC are some of the leading banks which deals in Personal Loan.

Almost all the banks have jumped into the market of car loan which is also sometimes termed as auto loan. It is one of the fast moving financial product of banks. Car loan / auto loan are sanctioned to the extent of 85% upon the ex-showroom price of the car with some simple paper works and a small amount of processing fee.

Loan against shares is very easy to get because liquid guarantee is involved in it.

Home loan is the latest craze in the banking sector with the development of the infrastructure. Now people are moving to township outside the city. More number of townships are coming up to meet the demand of 'house for all'. The RBI has also liberalised the interest rates of home loan inorder to match the repayment capability of even middle class people. Almost all banks are dealing in home loan. Again SBI, ICICI, HDFC, HSBC are leading.

The educational loan, rather to be termed as student loan, is a good banking product for the mass. Students with certain academic brilliance, studying at recognised colleges/

universities in India and abroad are generally given education loan / student loan so as to meet the expenses on tuition fee/ maintenance cost/books and other equipment.

MONEY TRANSFER

Beside lending and depositing money, banks also carry money from one corner of the globe to another. This act of banks is known as transfer of money. This activity is termed as remittance business. Banks generally issue Demand Drafts, Banker's Cheques, Money Orders or other such instruments for transferring the money. This is a type of Telegraphic Transfer or Tele Cash Orders.

It has been only a couple of years that banks have jumped into the money transfer businessess in India. The international money transfer market grew 9.3% from 2003 to 2004 i.e. from US$213 bn. to US$233 bn. in 2004. Economists say that the market of money transfer will further grow at a cumulative 10.1% average growth rate through 2008.

With the use of high technology and varieties of product it seems that "Free" money transfers will become commonplace. We will see more bundling of tailored money services by banks and non-traditional entrants that will include "free" money transfers. Many banks will even use money transfer services as loss-leaders inorder to generate account openings and cross-sell opportunities. The price evolution of money transfer products for banks will be similar to that of consumer bill pay- the product is worth giving away as an account acquisition tool to win overall market share and establish banking relationships.

ATM money transfer card products have had terrible bank adoption rates since being introduced in the last three to four years. Remittees who are highly educated and have been already been exposed to ATM technology in receiving countries tend to have an interest in this product. Money transfer to India is one of the most important part played by the banks. This service provide peace of mind to either the NRIs or to the visitors to India. Many Indian banks have ATM'S (automatic teller machine), enable to draw foreign currency in India.

By 2007, we will see a good percent of all foreign-born households doing some level of online banking. First-mover banks will start having a window of opportunity to include online transfer functionality within the next couple of years, which currently frequents traditional money transmitters such as Western Union.

There is a terrific opportunity for banks and non-banks to offer more robust global inter-institutional funds transfer services online. More than half of Western Union's customers today are already banked, and most do not have an alternative product marketed by their bank that is painless, quick, and cost-effective. That will change as banks offer transfer services through their online channel.

Money Transfer to India

Apart from banks few financial institutions and online portals gives services of money transfer to India. Some of them are as under:

- Western Union Money Transfer
- Union Money Transfer
- IKobo Money Transfer
- Cash2india.com
- Remit2india
- Samachar Money Transfer
- Timesofmoney.com
- Wells Fergo International Money Transfer
- Travellers Express
- Money Gram International

VISA MONEY TRANSFER

Visa has recently introduced the 'Visa Money Transfer' option for its savings and current account holder of any bank with a visa debit card. This facility helps its customer to transfer funds from his bank account to any visa card, either debit or credit within India.

A Visa Money Transfer is of similar kind, in many respects, to the third-party fund transfer option given by some banks to its account holders through e-cheque, but this is restricted to only visa cardholders.

How to Transfer Money?

- Log on to your bank account through your respective bank websites.
- Fill the beneficiary details like visa card numbers, name, address and then specify the amount that needs to be transferred. For bank account specify the visa card number and credit card number for paying credit card bill.
- Click on to VISA Transfer Payments button.
- Transfer immediately or on schedule date. Your account will be debited according to the date mentioned.

Notable points of Visa Money Transfer

- The time taken for money transfers could be the same or even more than that of a demand draft i.e. two or three days or even more.
- Currently there are no charges but limits has been set by certain banks on the current transfers.
- It is available in 150 cities across the country now.
- The transferred amount can neither be changed nor stopped once it is initiated.

4

Financial and Banking Sector Reforms

INTRODUCTION

In the last decade, Private Sector Institutions played an important role. They grew rapidly in commercial banking and asset management business. With the openings in the insurance sector for these institutions, they started making debt in the market. Competition among financial intermediaries gradually helped the interest rates to decline. Deregulation added to it. The real interest rate was maintained. The borrowers did not pay high price while depositors had incentives to save. It was something between the nominal rate of interest and the expected rate of inflation.

The last decade witnessed the maturity of India's financial markets. Since 1991, every governments of India took major steps in reforming the financial sector of the country. The important achievements in the following fields is discussed under serparate heads:

- Financial markets
- Regulators
- The banking system
- Non-banking finance companies

- The capital market
- Mutual funds
- Overall approach to reforms
- Deregulation of banking system
- Capital market developments
- Consolidation imperative

Now let us discuss each segment seperately.

FINANCIAL MARKETS REGULATORS

The Finance Ministry continuously formulated major policies in the field of financial sector of the country. The Government accepted the important role of regulators. The Reserve Bank of India (RBI) has become more independant. Securities and Exchange Board of India (SEBI) and the Insurance Regulatory and Development Authority (IRDA) became important institutions. Opinions are also there that there should be a super-regulator for the financial services sector instead of multiplicity of regulators.

The Banking System

Almost 80% of the business are still controlled by Public Sector Banks (PSBs). PSBs are still dominating the commercial banking system. Shares of the leading PSBs are already listed on the stock exchanges.

The RBI has given licences to new private sector banks as part of the liberalisation process. The RBI has also been granting licences to industrial houses. Many banks are successfully running in the retail and consumer segments but are yet to deliver services to industrial finance, retail trade, small business and agricultural finance.

The PSBs will play an important role in the industry due to its number of branches and foreign banks facing the constrait of limited number of branches. Hence, in order to achieve an efficient banking system, the onus is on the Government to encourage the PSBs to be run on professional lines.

Development Finance Institutions

FIs's access to SLR funds reduced. Now they have to approach the capital market for debt and equity funds.

Convertibility clause no longer obligatory for assistance to corporates sanctioned by term-lending institutions.

Capital adequacy norms extended to financial institutions.

DFIs such as IDBI and ICICI have entered other segments of financial services such as commercial banking, asset management and insurance through separate ventures. The move to universal banking has started.

Non-banking Finance Companies

In the case of new NBFCs seeking registration with the RBI, the requirement of minimum net owned funds, has been raised to Rs.2 crores.

Until recently, the money market in India was narrow and circumscribed by tight regulations over interest rates and participants. The secondary market was underdeveloped and lacked liquidity. Several measures have been initiated and include new money market instruments, strengthening of existing instruments and setting up of the Discount and Finance House of India (DFHI).

The RBI conducts its sales of dated securities and treasury bills through its open market operations (OMO) window. Primary dealers bid for these securities and also trade in them. The DFHI is the principal agency for developing a secondary market for money market instruments and Government of India treasury bills. The RBI has introduced a liquidity adjustment facility (LAF) in which liquidity is injected through reverse repo auctions and liquidity is sucked out through repo auctions.

On account of the substantial issue of government debt, the gilt- edged market occupies an important position in the financial set- up. The Securities Trading Corporation of India (STCI), which started operations in June 1994 has a mandate to develop the secondary market in government securities.

Long-term debt market: The development of a long-term debt market is crucial to the financing of infrastructure. After bringing some order to the equity market, the SEBI has now decided to concentrate on the development of the debt market. Stamp duty is being withdrawn at the time of dematerialisation of debt instruments in order to encourage paperless trading.

The Capital Market

The number of shareholders in India is estimated at 25 million. However, only an estimated two lakh persons actively trade in stocks. There has been a dramatic improvement in the country's stock market trading infrastructure during the last few years. Expectations are that India will be an attractive emerging market with tremendous potential. Unfortunately, during recent times the stock markets have been constrained by some unsavoury developments, which has led to retail investors deserting the stock markets.

Mutual Funds

The mutual funds industry is now regulated under the SEBI (Mutual Funds) Regulations, 1996 and amendments thereto. With the issuance of SEBI guidelines, the industry had a framework for the establishment of many more players, both Indian and foreign players.

The Unit Trust of India remains easily the biggest mutual fund controlling a corpus of nearly Rs.70,000 crores, but its share is going down. The biggest shock to the mutual fund industry during recent times was the insecurity generated in the minds of investors regarding the US 64 scheme. With the growth in the securities markets and tax advantages granted for investment in mutual fund units, mutual funds started becoming popular.

The foreign owned AMCs are the ones which are now setting the pace for the industry. They are introducing new products, setting new standards of customer service, improving disclosure standards and experimenting with new types of distribution.

The insurance industry is the latest to be thrown open to competition from the private sector including foreign players. Foreign companies can only enter joint ventures with Indian companies, with participation restricted to 26 per cent of equity. It is too early to conclude whether the erstwhile public sector monopolies will successfully be able to face up to the competition posed by the new players, but it can be expected that the customer will gain from improved service.

The new players will need to bring in innovative products as well as fresh ideas on marketing and distribution, in order to improve the low per capita insurance coverage. Good regulation will, of course, be essential.

Overall Approach to Reforms

The last ten years have seen major improvements in the working of various financial market participants. The government and the regulatory authorities have followed a step-by-step approach, not a big bang one. The entry of foreign players has assisted in the introduction of international practices and systems. Technology developments have improved customer service.

Some gaps however remain (for example: lack of an inter-bank interest rate benchmark, an active corporate debt market and a developed derivatives market). On the whole, the cumulative effect of the developments since 1991 has been quite encouraging. An indication of the strength of the reformed Indian financial system can be seen from the way India was not affected by the Southeast Asian crisis.

However, financial liberalisation alone will not ensure stable economic growth. Some tough decisions still need to be taken. Without fiscal control, financial stability cannot be ensured.

The fate of the Fiscal Responsibility Bill remains unknown and high fiscal deficits continue. In the case of financial institutions, the political and legal structures hve to ensure that borrowers repay on time the loans they have taken.

The phenomenon of rich industrialists and bankrupt companies continues. Further, frauds cannot be totally prevented, even with the best of regulation. However, punishment has to follow crime, which is often not the case in India.

DEREGULATION OF BANKING SYSTEM

Prudential norms were introduced for income recognition, asset classification, provisioning for delinquent loans and for capital adequacy. In order to reach the stipulated capital adequacy norms, substantial capital were provided by the Government to PSBs.

Government pre-emption of banks' resources through statutory liquidity ratio (SLR) and cash reserve ratio (CRR) brought down in steps. Interest rates on the deposits and lending sides almost entirely were deregulated.

New private sector banks allowed to promote and encourage competition. PSBs were encouraged to approach the public for raising resources. Recovery of debts due to banks and the Financial Institutions Act, 1993 was passed, and special recovery tribunals set up to facilitate quicker recovery of loan arrears.

Bank lending norms liberalised and a loan system to ensure better control over credit introduced. Banks asked to set up asset liability management (ALM) systems. RBI guidelines issued for risk management systems in banks encompassing credit, market and operational risks.

A credit information bureau being established to identify bad risks. Derivative products such as forward rate agreements (FRAs) and interest rate swaps (IRSs) introduced.

Capital Market Developments

The Capital Issues (Control) Act, 1947, repealed, office of the Controller of Capital Issues were abolished and the initial share pricing were decontrolled. SEBI, the capital market regulator was established in 1992.

Foreign institutional investors (FIIs) were allowed to invest in Indian capital markets after registration with the SEBI. Indian companies were permitted to access international capital markets through euro issues.

The National Stock Exchange (NSE), with nationwide stock trading and electronic display, clearing and settlement facilities was established. Several local stock exchanges changed over from floor based trading to screen based trading.

Private Mutual Funds Permitted

The Depositories Act had given a legal framework for the establishment of depositories to record ownership deals in book entry form. Dematerialisation of stocks encouraged paperless trading. Companies were required to disclose all material facts and specific risk factors associated with their projects while making public issues.

To reduce the cost of issue, underwriting by the issuer were made optional, subject to conditions. The practice of making preferential allotment of shares at prices unrelated to the prevailing market prices stopped and fresh guidelines were issued by SEBI.

SEBI reconstituted governing boards of the stock exchanges, introduced capital adequacy norms for brokers, and made rules for making client or broker relationship more transparent which included separation of client and broker accounts.

Buy Back of Shares Allowed

The SEBI started insisting on greater corporate disclosures. Steps were taken to improve corporate governance based on the report of a committee.

SEBI issued detailed employee stock option scheme and employee stock purchase scheme for listed companies. Standard denomination for equity shares of Rs. 10 and Rs. 100 were abolished. Companies given the freedom to issue dematerialised shares in any denomination. Derivatives trading starts with index options and futures. A system of rolling settlements introduced. SEBI empowered to register and regulate venture capital funds.

The SEBI (Credit Rating Agencies) Regulations, 1999 issued for regulating new credit rating agencies as well as introducing a code of conduct for all credit rating agencies operating in India.

Consolidation Imperative

Another aspect of the financial sector reforms in India is the consolidation of existing institutions which is especially applicable to the commercial banks. In India the banks are in huge quantity. First, there is no need for 27 PSBs with branches all over India. A number of them can be merged. The merger of Punjab National Bank and New Bank of India was a difficult one, but the situation is different now. No one expected so many employees to take voluntary retirement from PSBs, which at one time were much sought after jobs. Private sector banks will be self consolidated while co-operative and rural banks will be encouraged for consolidation, and anyway play only a niche role.

In the case of insurance, the Life Insurance Corporation of India is a behemoth, while the four public sector general insurance companies will probably move towards consolidation with a bit of nudging. The UTI is yet again a big institution, even though facing difficult times, and most other public sector players are already exiting the mutual fund business. There are a number of small mutual fund players in the private sector, but the business being comparatively new for the private players, it will take some time.

We finally come to convergence in the financial sector, the new buzzword internationally. Hi-tech and the need to meet increasing consumer needs is encouraging convergence, even though it has not always been a success till date. In India organisations such as IDBI, ICICI, HDFC and SBI are already trying to offer various services to the customer under one umbrella. This phenomenon is expected to grow rapidly in the coming years. Where mergers may not be possible, alliances between organisations may be effective. Various forms of bancassurance are being introduced, with the RBI having already come out with detailed guidelines for entry of banks into insurance.

The LIC has bought into Corporation Bank in order to spread its insurance distribution network. Both banks and insurance companies have started entering the asset management business, as there is a great deal of synergy among these businesses. The pensions market is expected to open up fresh opportunities for insurance companies and mutual funds.

It is not possible to play the role of the Oracle of Delphi when a vast nation like India is involved. However, a few trends are evident, and the coming decade should be as interesting as the last one.

RESERVE BANK OF INDIA (RBI)

The central bank of the country is the Reserve Bank of India (RBI). It was established in April 1935 with a share capital of Rs. 5 crores on the basis of the recommendations of the Hilton Young Commission. The share capital was divided into shares of Rs. 100 each fully paid which was entirely owned by private shareholders in the begining. The Government held shares of nominal value of Rs. 2,20,000.

Reserve Bank of India was nationalised in the year 1949. The general superintendence and direction of the Bank is entrusted to Central Board of Directors of 20 members, the Governor and four Deputy Governors, one Government official from the Ministry of Finance, ten nominated Directors by the Government to give representation to important elements in the economic life of the country, and four nominated Directors by the Central Government to represent the four local Boards with the headquarters at Mumbai, Kolkata, Chennai and New Delhi. Local Boards consist of five members each Central Government appointed for a term of four years to represent territorial and economic interests and the interests of co-operative and indigenous banks.

The Reserve Bank of India Act, 1934 was commenced on April 1, 1935. The Act, 1934 (II of 1934) provides the statutory basis of the functioning of the Bank.

The Bank was constituted for the need of following:

- To regulate the issue of banknotes
- To maintain reserves with a view to securing monetary stability and
- To operate the credit and currency system of the country to its advantage.

Functions of Reserve Bank of India

The Reserve Bank of India Act of 1934 entrust all the important functions of a central bank the Reserve Bank of India.

Bank of Issue

Under Section 22 of the Reserve Bank of India Act, the Bank has the sole right to issue bank notes of all denominations. The distribution of one rupee notes and coins and small coins all over the country is undertaken by the Reserve Bank as agent of the Government. The Reserve Bank has a separate

Issue Department which is entrusted with the issue of currency notes. The assets and liabilities of the Issue Department are kept separate from those of the Banking Department. Originally, the assets of the Issue Department were to consist of not less than two-fifths of gold coin, gold bullion or sterling securities provided the amount of gold was not less than Rs. 40 crores in value. The remaining three-fifths of the assets might be held in rupee coins, Government of India rupee securities, eligible bills of exchange and promissory notes payable in India. Due to the exigencies of the Second World War and the post-was period, these provisions were considerably modified. Since 1957, the Reserve Bank of India is required to maintain gold and foreign exchange reserves of Ra. 200 crores, of which at least Rs. 115 crores should be in gold. The system as it exists today is known as the minimum reserve system.

Banker to Government

The second important function of the Reserve Bank of India is to act as Government banker, agent and adviser. The Reserve Bank is agent of Central Government and of all State Governments in India excepting that of Jammu and Kashmir. The Reserve Bank has the obligation to transact Government business, via. to keep the cash balances as deposits free of interest, to receive and to make payments on behalf of the Government and to carry out their exchange remittances and other banking operations. The Reserve Bank of India helps the Government - both the Union and the States to float new loans and to manage public debt. The Bank makes ways and means advances to the Governments for 90 days. It makes loans and advances to the States and local authorities. It acts as adviser to the Government on all monetary and banking matters.

Bankers' Bank and Lender of the Last Resort

The Reserve Bank of India acts as the bankers' bank. According to the provisions of the Banking Companies Act of 1949, every scheduled bank was required to maintain with the

Reserve Bank a cash balance equivalent to 5% of its demand liabilites and 2 per cent of its time liabilities in India. By an amendment of 1962, the distinction between demand and time liabilities was abolished and banks have been asked to keep cash reserves equal to 3 per cent of their aggregate deposit liabilities. The minimum cash requirements can be changed by the Reserve Bank of India.

The scheduled banks can borrow from the Reserve Bank of India on the basis of eligible securities or get financial accommodation in times of need or stringency by rediscounting bills of exchange. Since commercial banks can always expect the Reserve Bank of India to come to their help in times of banking crisis the Reserve Bank becomes not only the banker's bank but also the lender of the last resort.

Controller of Credit

The Reserve Bank of India is the controller of credit i.e. it has the power to influence the volume of credit created by banks in India. It can do so through changing the Bank rate or through open market operations. According to the Banking Regulation Act of 1949, the Reserve Bank of India can ask any particular bank or the whole banking system not to lend to particular groups or persons on the basis of certain types of securities. Since 1956, selective controls of credit are increasingly being used by the Reserve Bank.

The Reserve Bank of India is armed with many more powers to control the Indian money market. Every bank has to get a licence from the Reserve Bank of India to do banking business within India, the licence can be cancelled by the Reserve Bank of certain stipulated conditions are not fulfilled. Every bank will have to get the permission of the Reserve Bank before it can open a new branch.

Each scheduled bank must send a weekly return to the Reserve Bank showing, in detail, its assets and liabilities. This power of the Bank to call for information is also intended to give it effective control of the credit system. The Reserve Bank has also the power to inspect the accounts of any commercial bank.

As supereme banking authority in the country, the Reserve Bank of India, therefore, has the following powers:

(a) It holds the cash reserves of all the scheduled banks.

(b) It controls the credit operations of banks through quantitative and qualitative controls.

(c) It controls the banking system through the system of licensing, inspection and calling for information.

(d) It acts as the lender of the last resort by providing rediscount facilities to scheduled banks.

Custodian of Foreign Reserves

The Reserve Bank of India has the responsibility to maintain the official rate of exchange. According to the Reserve Bank of India Act of 1934, the Bank was required to buy and sell at fixed rates any amount of sterling in lots of not less than Rs. 10,000. The rate of exchange fixed was Re. 1 = sh. 6d. Since 1935 the Bank was able to maintain the exchange rate fixed at lsh.6d. though there were periods of extreme pressure in favour of or against the rupee. After India became a member of the International Monetary Fund in 1946, the Reserve Bank has the responsibility of maintaining fixed exchange rates with all other member countries of the I.M.F.

Besides maintaining the rate of exchange of the rupee, the Reserve Bank has to act as the custodian of India's reserve of international currencies. The vast sterling balances were acquired and managed by the Bank. Further, the RBI has the responsibility of administering the exchange controls of the country.

Supervisory Functions

In addition to its traditional central banking functions, the Reserve bank has certain non-monetary functions of the nature of supervision of banks and promotion of sound banking in India. The Reserve Bank Act, 1934, and the Banking Regulation Act, 1949 have given the RBI wide powers of supervision and control over commercial and co-operative banks, relating to licensing and establishments, branch expansion, liquidity of their assets, management and methods of working, amalgamation, reconstruction, and liquidation. The RBI is authorised to carry out periodical inspections of the banks and to call for returns and necessary information from them. The nationalisation of 14 major Indian scheduled banks in July 1969 has imposed new responsibilities on the RBI for directing the growth of banking and credit policies towards more rapid development of the economy and realisation of certain desired social objectives. The supervisory functions of the RBI have helped a great deal in improving the standard of banking in India to develop on sound lines and to improve the methods of their operation.

Promotional Functions

With economic growth assuming a new urgency since Independence, the range of the Reserve Bank's functions has steadily widened. The Bank now performs a varietyof developmental and promotional functions, which, at one time, were regarded as outside the normal scope of central banking. The Reserve Bank was asked to promote banking habit, extend banking facilities to rural and semi-urban areas, and establish and promote new specialised financing agencies. Accordingly, the Reserve Bank has helped in the setting up of the IFCI and the SFC; it set up the Deposit Insurance Corporation in 1962, the Unit Trust of India in 1964, the Industrial Development Bank of India also in 1964, the Agricultural Refinance Corporation of India in 1963 and the Industrial Reconstruction Corporation of India in 1972. These institutions were set up directly or indirectly by the Reserve Bank to promote saving habit and to mobilise savings, and to provide industrial finance as well as agricultural finance.

As far back as 1935, the Reserve Bank of India set up the Agricultural Credit Department to provide agricultural credit. But only since 1951 the Bank's role in this field has become extremely important. The Bank has developed the co-operative credit movement to encourage saving, to eliminate moneylenders from the villages and to route its short term credit to agriculture. The RBI has set up the Agricultural Refinance and Development Corporation to provide long-term finance to farmers.

CLASSIFICATION OF RBIS FUNCTIONS

The monetary functions also known as the central banking functions of the RBI are related to control and regulation of money and credit, i.e., issue of currency, control of bank credit, control of foreign exchange operations, banker to the Government and to the money market. Monetary functions of the RBI are significant as they control and regulate the volume of money and credit in the country.

Equally important, however, are the non-monetary functions of the RBI in the context of India's economic backwardness. The supervisory function of the RBI may be regarded as a non-monetary function (though many consider this a monetary function).

The promotion of sound banking in India is an important goal of the RBI, the RBI has been given wide and drastic powers, under the Banking Regulation Act of 1949 - these powers relate to licencing of banks, branch expansion, liquidity of their assets, management and methods of working, inspection, amalgamation, reconstruction and liquidation. Under the RBI's supervision and inspection, the working of banks has greatly improved. Commercial banks have developed into financially and operationally sound and viable units.

The RBI's powers of supervision have now been extended to non-banking financial intermediaries. Since independence, particularly after its nationalisation 1949, the RBI has followed the promotional functions vigorously and has been responsible for strong financial support to industrial and agricultural development in the country.

INDUSTRIAL DEVELOPMENT BANK OF INDIA LTD. (IDBI)

Industrial Development Bank of India (IDBI) is the tength largest bank in the world in terms of development. The National Stock Exchange (NSE), The National Securities Depository Services Ltd. (NSDL), Stock Holding Corporation of India (SHCIL) are some of the institutions which has been built by IDBI. IDBI is a strategic investor in a plethora of institutions which have revolutionized the Indian Financial Markets.

IDBI Bank, promoted by IDBI Group started in November 1995 with a branch at Indore with an equity capital base of Rs. 1000 million.

Main Functions of IDBI

IDBI is vested with the responsibility of co-ordinating the working of institutions engaged in financing, promoting and developing industries. It has evolved an appropriate mechanism for this purpose.

IDBI also undertakes/supports wide-ranging promotional activities including entrepreneurship development programmes for new entrepreneurs, provision of consultancy services for small and medium enterprises, upgradation of technology and programmes for economic upliftment of the underprivileged.

IDBI's Role as a Catalyst

IDBI's role as a catalyst to industrial development encompasses a wide spectrum of activities. IDBI can finance all types of industrial concerns covered under the provisions of the IDBI Act.

With over three decades of service to the Indian industry, IDBI has grown substantially in terms of size of operations and portfolio.

Developmental Activities of IDBI

Promotional Activities

In fulfilment of its developmental role, the Bank continues to perform a wide range of promotional activities relating to developmental programmes for new entrepreneurs, consultancy services for small and medium enterprises and programmes designed for accredited voluntary agencies for the economic upliftment of the underprivileged.

These include entrepreneurship development, self-employment and wage employment in the industrial sector for the weaker sections of society through voluntary agencies, support to Science and Technology Entrepreneurs' Parks, Energy Conservation, Common Quality Testing Centres for small industries.

Technical Consultancy Organisations

With a view to making available at a reasonable cost, consultancy and advisory services to entrepreneurs, particularly to new and small entrepreneurs, IDBI, in collaboration with other All-India Financial Institutions, has set up a network of Technical Consultancy Organisations (TCOs) covering the entire country. TCOs offer diversified services to small and medium enterprises in the selection, formulation and appraisal of projects, their implementation and review.

Entrepreneurship Development Institute

Realising that entrepreneurship development is the key to industrial development, IDBI played a prime role in setting up of the Entrepreneurship Development Institute of India for fostering entrepreneurship in the country.

It has also established similar institutes in Bihar, Orissa, Madhya Pradesh and Uttar Pradesh. IDBI also extends financial support to various organisations in conducting studies or surveys of relevance to industrial development.

EASY BANKING

This section is fully dedicated to the Tech Banking. A decade before, it was tough to belief that banking secctor will be at a finger tip. Now its possible. A mobile hand set with a connection is the only instrument needed to make a gateway to your banking transaction, the latest innovation of technology.

Apart from the Mobile Banking, including of SMS Banking, Net Banking and ATMs are the major steps taken by the banks in India towards modernisation. With all these devises and systems, there is a complete freedom to experience.

Check your account, transfer your fund, make payments and what more, do anything of everything what has been followed in physical banking since ages. But this time no standing for hours in front of cash counter and no time boundation in withdrawing your own money.

AUTOMATED TELLER MACHINE (ATM)

The first bank to introduce the ATM concept in India was the Hongkong and Shanghai Banking Corporation (HSBC). It was in the year 1987. Now, almost every commercial banks gives ATM facilities to its customers.

The first bank to cross 1,000 marks in installing ATMs in India is ICICI. SBI is following the concept of 'ATMs in Quantity'. But Private Sector Banks have taken the lead. ICICI, UTI, HDFC and IDBI counts more than 50% of the total ATMs in India.

Public Sector Banks are also taking the installation of ATMs seriously for Indian market. They are either setting up their own ATM centres or entering into tie-ups with other banks. The Corporation Bank has the second largest network of ATMs amongst the Public Sector Banks in India.

The Indian banks have also come up with a 'Swadhan' scheme. Under this scheme, the banks can use each other's ATM at a cost, usually Rs. 35 extra from their customers. The main feature of 'Swadhan Card' are as follows:

- No exchange fee charged to change an old ATM card for a Swadhan card.
- Rs. 3,000 fixed as the ceiling on withdrawal.
- Exception made for select customers who can withdraw up to Rs10,000. Still, this is lower than the average withdrawal of Rs15,000 by regular ATMs.
- IBA gives banks the discretion to decide a higher maximum amount for withdrawal.
- Transactions conducted through any of the member banks appear on a bank statement, which is given only by your own bank.
- All transactions conducted in any of the member banks appear on the bank statement, but only your own bank will provide this.

Note :- No overdraft facility is available on Swadhan cards.

How 'Swadhan Card' Works

All informations and transactions are routed among member institutions through a switch. The switch transmits the information and/or data to bank which has issued the card or to its processor, which on the other hand either approves or declines the transaction request and notifies the switch.

The decision of the card-issuing bank's is then routed by the switch to the processor of the ATM, which completes the transaction. The accounts among members are settled and account balances are transmitted at the end of the day to each member institution.

Cost of Setting ATM Center

Approximately Rs.1mn it takes for the setting of an ATM center. Rs.1.2-1.4mn per annum is needed for its maintenance. To keep the cost in equilibrium position, there should be around 250-300 transactions per day per ATM.

To overcome or to reach the break-even point, the banks are always encouraging its customers to use the ATMs. Banks like HDFC and Citibank even charge penalty if a customer visits the branch.

NCR India and HMA Die bold are the main two players in this market to set up ATMs in India. The market, according to them is whopping 100% and they are very optimistic to see 30,000 ATMs in India very soon.

5

Net and Mobile Banking

INTRODUCTION

The regulatory body has not yet sanctioned virtual bank, in abroad there are banks like EGG Bank or NET Bank, which only have a virtual presence without any physical branches. Net Banking is conducting ones banking or bank account online through a computer and a net connection. The system is updated immediately after every transaction automatically. In other words it is said that it is updated 'on-line, real time'. Through netbanking one can check the status of his/her account, place queries and also can be facilitated with a wide range of transactions simultaneously.

Net Banking has three basic features. They are as follows:

- The banks offer only relevant informations about their products and services to the mass.
- Few banks provide interaction facility between the banks and its customers.
- Banks are coming up with arrangements of utility payments, like telephone bills, electricity bills, etc.

The current statistics show that hardly 10 per cent of Indian customers uses the internet for banking. Among all the facilities provided, the maximum of them uses only for checking balance or requesting for a cheque book. Very few customers uses the advance interactive services provided by the banks.

According to HDFC and ICICI Bank, 17 per cent of ICICI customers use the Internet for banking and 10 per cent of HDFC customers prefer it.

Cost of Installation of Services

For basic features, the cost for providing such services to the banks come around Rs 40 lakh to Rs 50 lakh. For the third level service or sophisticated services, the investments mount to the tune of Rs 4 crore to Rs 5 crore. These investments is just a fraction if compared to the operations of the bank using physical infrastructure.

MOBILE BANKING

"The account that travels with you". This is needed in today's fast business environment with unending deadlines for fulfillment and loads of appointments to meed and meetings to attend. With mobile banking facilities, one can bank from anywhere, at anytime and in any condition or anyhow. The system is either through SMS or through WAP. (Check out for SMS Banking under different head)

Mobile Banking is the hottest area of development in the banking sector and is expected to replace the credit/debit card system in future. In past two years, mobile banking users has increased three times if we compare the use of either debit card or credit card. Moveover 85-90% mobile users do not own credit cards.

Mobile banking uses the same infrastructure like the ATM solution. But it is extremely easy and inexpensive to implement. It reduces the cost of operation for bankers in comparison to the use of ATMs.

Using compact HTML and WAP technologies, the following operations can be conducted through advanced mobile phones which can is further viewed on channels such as the Internet via the Channel Manager.

- Bill payments
- Fund transfers
- Check balances
- Any many more which is also available in SMS Banking

In countries like Korea, two SIM Card is used in mobile phones. One for the telephonic purpose and the other for banking. Bank account data is encrypted on a smart-card chip. About 3.3 million transactions were reported by Bank of Korea in 2004.

SMS BANKING

Businesses are in move. So is to be your money. You may have to thank the banks which are providing banking at the send-of-your-sms. The technology is at its highest level to move your money while you are on the move. If you are having non-WAP enabled mobile handset, you can use the facility of SMS services. The following operations can be easily used by the service provider:

- Balance enquiry
- Last three transactions
- Cheque payment status
- Cheque book request
- Statement request
- Demat - Free Balance Holding
- Demat - Last two Transactions
- Bill Payment

The SMS facility brings peace of mind to customers and opens doors to many more technological possibilities and innovative services. It is very similar to how an ATM works.

To use ATM, a card is necessary and to use SMS service, a mobile phone is needed. In both the cases, secret number is necessary to access.

SMS banking is also very much safe. First, one authenticates the mobile number with the authentications key. Second, the customer uses secret Mobile Personal Iddentification Number (MPIN).

A new concept has been developed by Bank of Punjab Ltd. They call it "Mobile Wallet". With the support of this technology, a customer can make payment and receive payment of account of buy/sell (merchants) through SMS.

In this system, a buyer sends a message for buying and the bank in return sends a message confirming the purchase both to the merchant as well as to the buyer. Debit card number is the key field which is used for the authenticity of the customer.

The processes of the service are simplified as under:

- Customer has to send "REG(one space)(Account Number)(one space)(Debit Card Number)" as an SMS to bank's mobile number 9810999992 for registration. For e.g. "REG 06SB11052122 5047531105000109109" Bank will confirm the registration with the return message.
- After that customer will visit nearest branch to collect the service brochure and get it filled.
- Registration will be a one time process.Once registered, customer would be able to buy things from any of the registered merchant of the bank.
- Customer need to send "PAY(one space)(merchant code)(one space)(amount)(one space)(Debit card number)" as an SMS on bank's mobile number 9810999992. For e.g for making a payment of Rs. 56.16 to merchant BOPSTC from card no. 5047531105000109109, Send the following message "PAY BOPSTC 56.16 5047531105000109109"

- The transaction will be validated online and immediately funds will be transferred from customer account to merchant account.
- Bank would send transaction confirmation as an message to both merchant and customer(buyer).
- An SMS report will be sent to both merchant & buyer everyday stating the total number of transaction & total amount of transaction made during previous one day.

Note :- There is obviously a limit to the volume of transactions now.

SOME USEFUL TIPS

Generally with 3 invalid login attempts, SMS Banking services are locked. Immediately contact the branch for unlocking the services. In case one forgets the password, obtain a new password from the branch. To log out, choose the "Log out" option in the handset and SMS Banking session ends.

Services Provided by Net Banking

Queries

- Check Balance
- See Statement
- Inquire about cheque status
- Ask for a Statement
- Ask for a Cheque Book
- Inquire about Fixed Deposit
- Inquire about TDS details
- See Demat Account
- Update profile

Transactions

- Stop a Cheque

- Pay Bills
- Ask for a Demand Draft
- Transfer funds between your accounts
- Transfer funds to a third party
- Request for a new Fixed Deposit
- Shop Online
- Pay Bank Credit Card Dues

Advantages of Net Banking

- It removes the traditional geographical barriers as it could reach out to customers of different countries/ legal jurisdiction. This has raised the question of jurisdiction of law/supervisory system to which such transactions should be subjected.
- It has added a new dimension to different kinds of risks traditionally associated with banking, heightening some of them and throwing new risk control challenges.
- Security of banking transactions, validity of electronic contract, customers' privacy, etc., which have all along been concerns of both bankers and supervisors have assumed different dimensions given that Internet is a public domain, not subject to control by any single authority or group of users.
- It poses a strategic risk of loss of business to those banks who do not respond in time to this new technology, being the efficient and cost effective delivery.

BANKING SERVICES FOR NRIS IN INDIA

Almost all the Indian Banks provide services to the NRIs. There are different types of accounts for them. They are:

- Non-Resident (Ordinary) Account - NRO A/c

- Non-Resident (External) Rupee Account - NRE A/c
- Non-Resident (Foreign Currency) Account - FCNR A/c

a.An Indian resident who is earning forign exchange can also maintain Foreign Currency account in the country with an authorised dealer bank but only to the maximum limit of 50% of such foreign exchange earnings under the Exchange Earners Foreign Currency Account (EEFC) Scheme.

Some of the FAQs given below will make it easy to understand the services provided by banks to the NRIs.

TOP BANKS IN INDIA

With the advancement of technology and the birth of competition, banks are in the race of becoming the best in the country.

With an eye upon customer satisfaction policy they are providing best of the best services with the minimum hazards. Banks like ABN AMRO introduced banking with a coffee.

It made a tie-up with one of the best coffee bar in the country, Barista and remained open till late evening for customers with a setup of a coffee bar in the premises.

Few banks have introduced world ATM card to make travellers across the globe more safe and secure. What else. Internet and Phone Banking is the call of the day for banks.

In this race towards the best, we have selected top 20 banks in the country from all segment. It is not the ranking of banks but only for general information about the top banks in India.

Indian Banks Association

The Indian Banks Association (IBA) was formed on the 26th September, 1946 with 22 members. Today IBA has more than 156 members comprising of Public Sector banks, Private Sector banks, Foreign banks having offices in India, Urban Cooperative banks, Developmental financial institutions, Federations, merchant banks, mutual funds, housing finance corporations, etc.

The Functioning of IBA

- To promote sound and progressive banking principles and practices.
- To render assistance and to provide common services to members.
- To organise co-ordination and co-operation on procedural, legal, technical, administrative and professional matters.
- To collect, classify and circulate statistical and other information.
- To pool together expertise towards common purposes such as reduction in costs, increase in efficiency, productivity and improve systems, procedures and banking practices.
- To project good public image of banking through publicity and public relations.
- To encourage sports and cultural activities among bank employees.

The Offices of IBA

The Organisational Structure of IBA

The Managing Committee manages the affairs, business and funds of IBA. The managing Committee is elected by the Ordinary members of the Association, and is the highest management and policy making body of the Association.

The Chairman of the Association heads upon the working of the Association. He provides guidelines to the Association. The administrative head of IBA is the Chief Executive of IBA. He is also the Secretary to the Managing Committee. He leads a team of executives, officers and other staff members. IBA constitutes standing committees/task forces/ small groups/ committees of experts from member banks for the examining of various aspects relating to industry level issues to get solutions. Recommendations of these groups/committees, are communicated to members with the approval of the managing committee or taken up with the concerned authorities for action.

PROXY BANKING IN INDIA

Indian villages were miles away from mutual funds, insurance and even equity trading. Thanks to Internet Kiosk and the ATM duo which has made it possible for rural India. This kiosk has been set up by ICICI Bank in partnership with network n-Logue Communications in remote villages of Southern part of the country.

This is known as Proxi Banking. With the help of fibre optic cables, this kiosk works on wireless in local loop technology.

Reasons for Setting-up of Proxi Banking

- 58% of rural households still do not have bank accounts.
- Only 21% of rural households have access to credit from a formal source.
- 70% of marginal farmers do not have deposit account.
- 87% households have no formal credit.
- Only 1% rural househlods rely on a loan from a financial intermediary. · The loans take between 24 to 33 weeks to get sanctioned.
- Consumers bribe officials to get loans approved which varies between 10 and 20 per cent of the loan amount.
- Branch banking in rurals is a loss-making.

Benefits to Rurals

- Small loans given for buying buffaloes

- Loans for setting up a tea shop.
- Life and non-life insurance provided.
- Weather insurance given to farmers.
- Insurance policies sold to farmers like groundnut, castor, soya, paddy crop, etc.

The Proxy Banking is an innovative approach to rural lending and will add to the government's expanding base of kisan credit cards and the good old guidelines for agricultural lending.

Bank of India was founded in 1906 in Mumbai. It became the first Indian bank to open a branch outside India in London in 1946 and the first to open a branch in continental Europe at Paris in 1974.

6

Economic Perspectives of Banking

INTRODUCTION

According to unconfirmed reports, the Reserve Bank of India (RBI) has approved a proposal from the government to amend the Banking Regulation Act to permit banks to trade in commodities and commodity derivatives. This offer to banks of one more new avenue of speculative investment by removal of a prohibition on commodity trading that has been in existence for long merely furthers the fundamental changes that have been under way in India's banking sector. The, banks seem to be the prime targets of the government's reforming zeal. Having encouraged foreign acquisition, consolidation and universalisation in the banking system, the Finance Ministry's current thrust seems to be to find a host of new areas of activity for these institutions. These changes impinge upon the nature of the institutions, operations and instruments that constitute the sector. Institutional changes include: a rapid increase in the number of new private sector banks; a process of consolidation of banks that thus far has principally affected the private banking sector but is now being consciously promoted in the public sector as well; privatisation of equity in public sector banks; mergers of banks and other financial institutions, particularly development banking institutions; and the creation of universal banks that are in the nature of financial supermarkets, offering customers a range of products from across the financial sector such as debt products, investment opportunities in equity, debt and commodity markets and insurance products of different kinds.

Implicit in these institutional changes are changes in the operations of the increasingly "universalised" banks. The most crucial change has been an increasing reluctance of banks to play their traditional role as agents who carry risks in return for a margin defined broadly by the spread between deposit and lending rates. Traditionally, banks accepted small deposits that highly liquid investments protected against capital and income risk. They in turn made large investments in highly illiquid assets characterised by a significant degree of capital and income risk. This made banks crucial intermediaries for facilitating the conversion of savings into investment.

Given this crucial role of intermediation conventionally reserved for the banking system, the regulatory framework that had the central bank at is apex, sought to protect the banking system from possible fragility and failure. That protective framework across the globe involved regulating interest rates, providing for deposit insurance and limiting the areas of activity and the investments undertaken by the banking system. The understanding was that banks should not divert household savings placed in their care to risky investments promising high returns. In developing countries, the interventionist framework also had developmental objectives and involved measures to direct credit to what were "priority" sectors in the government's view.

IN recent years, liberalisation and "denationalisation" have changed all that and forced a change in banking practices in two ways. First, private players are unsatisfied with returns that are available within a regulated framework, so that the government and the central bank have had to dilute or dismantle regulatory measures as is happening in the case of priority lending as well as restrictions on banking activities in India. Second, even public sector banks find that as private domestic and foreign banks, particularly the latter, lure away the most lucrative banking clients because of the special services and terms they are able to offer, they have to seek new sources of finance, new activities and new avenues for investments, so that they can shore up their interest incomes as well as revenues from various fee-based activities.

In sum, the processes of liberalisation fundamentally alter the terrain of operation of the banks. Their immediate impact is visible in a shift in the focus of bank activities away from facilitating commodity production and investment to lubricating trade and promoting personal consumption. Interest rates in these areas are much higher than that which could be charged to investments in commodity production. According to a study (Consumer Outlook 2004), conducted by market research firm KSA Technopak, Indian consumers are increasingly financing purchases of their dream products with credit that is now on offer, even without collateral. "Personal credit offtake has increased from about Rs.50,000 crores in 2000 to Rs.160,000 crores in 2003, giving an unprecedented boom to high-ticket item purchases such as housing and automobiles," the study reportedly found.

But there are changes also in the areas of operation of the banks, with banking entities not only creating or linking up with insurance companies, but also entering into other "sensitive" markets such as the stock and the real estate. It should be expected that this growing exposure to non-collateralised personal debt and entry into sensitive sectors would increase bank vulnerability to default or failure. The effects on bank fragility became clear after the stock scam of the late 1990s. RBI's Monetary and Credit Policy Statement for the year 2001-2002 had noted: "The recent experience in equity markets, and its aftermath, have thrown up new challenges for the regulatory system as well as for the conduct of monetary policy. It has become evident that certain banks in the cooperative sector did not adhere to their prudential norms nor to the well-defined regulatory guidelines for asset-liability management nor even to the requirement of meeting their inter-bank payment obligations. Even though such behaviour was confined to a few relatively small banks, by national standards, in two or three locations, it caused losses to some correspondent banks in addition to severe problems for depositors."

INTERESTINGLY, this increase in financial fragility has been accompanied by the emergence of new instruments in the banking sector. Derivatives of different kinds are now traded in the Indian financial system including, crucially, credit derivatives. Most derivatives, financial instruments whose value is based on or derived from the value of something else, are linked to interest rates or currencies. Credit derivatives are based on the value of loans, bonds or other lending instruments.

A working group of the RBI had recommended in 2003 that scheduled commercial banks may initially be permitted to use credit derivatives only for managing their credit risks. But banks were not permitted to take long or short credit derivative positions with a trading intent. Credit derivatives were seen as helping banks manage the risk arising from adverse movements in the quality of their loans, advances, and investments by transferring that risk to a protection seller. Using credit derivatives, banks can (1) transfer credit risk and, hence, free up capital, which can be used in other opportunities; (2) diversify credit risk; (3) maintain client relationships, and (4) construct and manage a credit risk portfolio as per their risk preference.

Banks in India have quickly responded to this opportunity. For example, soon after the introduction of interest rate futures in India, Citigroup concluded three securitisation deals worth Rs.570 crores ($126.6 billion), where yields on government securities or the call money rate, were used as the benchmark for pricing floating rate payments for investors. The underlying receivables arise from a large number of fixed rate loan contracts made for financing commercial vehicles and construction equipment. The risk here is being shared with mutual funds, who are reportedly the major investors.

Even the conservative State Bank of India (SBI) has taken a plunge into the credit derivatives market to cope with the risk arising from its growing loan portfolio.

The bank had recorded a growth of almost Rs.36,000 crores or 25 per cent in its loan portfolio on a year-on-year basis until September 2004, starting from a total loan assets position of Rs.135,000 crores in the corresponding period of the previous year. Of this credit growth, more than 40 per cent had been contributed by retail assets. Credit derivatives offered an opportunity to hedge against the risks being accumulated in this manner.

It should be clear that credit derivatives are an industry response to the increasing fragility that comes with the changed nature of banking practices. Derivatives of this kind permit the socialisation of the risks associated with the liberalisation-induced transformation of banking.

These trends are in keeping with changes in the international banking industry as well. As The Economist, London, put it: "The world's leading banks decided some years ago that lending is a mugs' game. They began to get rid of their loans, repackaging them and selling them off as securities, or getting others to re-insure their risk."

From the point of view of the banks this effort has been extremely fruitful. Thus, when there was a major melt down in corporate America, as a result of financial fraud and accounting malpractice, leading to the closure of giants like Enron and WorldCom, leading banks that had lent large sums to them appeared unaffected. According to one estimate, loans totalling $34 billion were wiped out through these bankruptcies. But far less amounts showed up as losses in the bank's accounts and, in the second quarter of 2003, Citigroup reported a 12 per cent increase in profits and J.P. Morgan Chase a 78 per cent increase. It should be clear that these losses have to show up somewhere in the accounts of the financial system, but as the

Bank of International Settlements (BIS) argued, its not easy to trace them.

"The markets lack transparency about the ultimate distribution of credit risks," it declared. One reason could be that these losses were being borne by insurance companies, which would be treating them like any other casualty loss so that they are not identifiable. The BIS sees this conundrum as being the result of the substantial growth of the practice of credit-risk transfer - the shifting of risk from banks on to the buyers of securities and loans, and on to the sellers of credit insurance.

IN sum, the traditional image of the great banks with armoured vaults has little to do with the banks of today. The latter appear to make loans and then pass them on as quickly as possible, pocketing the margin. That allows them to take bigger risks in trading securities, derivatives, and foreign exchange.

But these risks do not go away. At the end of 2002, though non-bank entities accounted for just 10 per cent of the syndicated loan market in the United States, they held 22.6 per cent of the bad or doubtful loans. The same is now happening in India, increasing the fragility of a host of non-bank financial institutions, such as pension funds, mutual funds and life-insurance companies.

Unfortunately, rather than recognise this danger, the Finance Ministry is keen on ensuring changes of the kind described above through a state-directed process of financial engineering. The full implications of the resulting changes would be revealed only in the days to come. But the experience elsewhere provides cause for concern.

INDIAN BANKING SYSTEM: GROWING AT AN ADMIRABLY FASTER PACE

Commendable growth has been witnessed in the financial system of India over the past few years. With a chain of more than 65,000 branches, Indian banking system is one of the largest banking networks in the world.

There has been a considerable growth in the retail-banking sector in India, which makes up for about 1/5th of the overall bank credit. Typically, the retail banking industry encompasses the services such as credit cards, housing loans, educational loans and auto loans etc.

Retail banking has brought in a drastic makeover in the overall banking scenario in India. The exceptional improvement in the banking system in India is a result of strong initiatives taken up by both the government and private companies.

A recent market research report named, "Indian Retail Banking Sector Analysis 2007" published by RNCOS provides an exclusive tour to the entire retail-banking industry of India.

As per the report, "Mainstream banking and retail banking have become one and the same thing for the past several years now. Approximately, 22% of the total outstanding advances were derived from the retail portfolios of the banks in India till March 2004".

"The contribution of retail banking to the overall banking sector has been outstanding. Growing at a rate of 122%, the retail-banking sector of India managed to reach a worth of $67 billion in the year 2005", as per experts at RNCOS. "The retail banking sector in India should reach a worth of $310 billion by the year 2010", anticipate the experts.

Profiles of key players along with the strategies and plans adopted by them for the growth of the industry are also talked about in it.

Besides discussing the present scenario of the financial system in India the report offers a reliable prediction of the market in the years to come. The report is extremely important for the investors and corporates, as it will help them make better strategies for the growth of their business.

INDIAN BANKING SYSTEM IMMUNE

The Indian banking system is better positioned today than ever before in terms of its business and financial health, notes a new CRISIL study. Says Arun Panicker, director, financial sector ratings at CRISIL, "The past few years have seen a continuous improvement in the key indicators of the banks' health, such as asset quality and capital adequacy." This is in alignment with the global banking trends: the performance of the banking sector has improved globally over the past few years.

According to Krishnan Sitaraman, head, financial sector ratings, "CRISIL has ratings outstanding on the debt instruments of 34 scheduled commercial banks; these banks account for 80 per cent of the Indian banking industry's assets. The outlooks, wherever assigned, are stable, on the expectation that the banks' credit will not change materially over the medium term." For the 21 rated public sector banks, CRISIL's ratings reflect the benefits of majority ownership by the government of India, which are expected to continue, and the banks' strong resource profiles.

CRISIL's recent banking sector analyses illustrate these conclusions through the following five commentaries:

- Impact of similarities with mid-90s manageable for banks: There are numerous superficial similarities between the mid-1990s and the mid-2000s, including money supply growth, credit growth, economic growth, industrial growth, and interest rate trends. However, CRISIL sees the underlying indicators pointing towards a substantial improvement in the current overall health of the banking system vis-à-vis the 1990s. Asset quality has improved significantly, with gross NPAs at less than 4 per cent of advances as on March 31, 2006, compared to 19.5 per cent as on March 31, 1995.

Similarly, the capitalisation levels of the scheduled commercial banks has also improved sharply from the mid-1990s, with the aggregate net worth increasing to Rs1,417 billion as on March 31, 2005, from Rs215 billion as on March 31, 1994, leaving them adequately capitalised on a systemic basis even for a stress scenario. Thus, although the deteriorating asset quality in the late 1990s had a severe impact on the banks' balance sheets, CRISIL believes that such a situation is unlikely to recur today.

- Banking sector liquidity manageable at systemic level: CRISIL's analysis reveals that, despite high credit growth rates, systemic liquidity is expected to be manageable in the medium term. In 2005-06 (refers to financial year, April 1 to March 31), the credit extended by the banking sector grew at a rapid 32 per cent, after a significant 26 per cent credit growth in 2004-05. The deposit growth of 15 per cent in 2005-06 was not sufficient to cover this increase. While bank deposits have not been losing out significantly to other sources of savings, the magnitude of credit growth has forced the banks to look to other sources of funds as well.

The gap between deposit growth and credit growth also resulted in some tightness in liquidity in the banking sector during the second half of 2005-06; banks have managed this tightness by selling off investments, and increasing bulk deposits. CRISIL believes that this tightness was a temporary phenomenon, and the aggregate liquidity situation in the banking sector is now manageable. CRISIL's analysis also reveals that a bank deposit growth of 16 per cent in 2006-07 will be sufficient from a systemic perspective to comfortably sustain credit growth of even 25 per cent, given the current structure of banks' balance sheets. Nevertheless, on a case-specific basis, there are banks that have low levels of excess statutory liquidity ratio (SLR) investments; in the absence of corresponding deposit growth, such banks would need bulk borrowings to meet the credit expansion.

- Banking sector asset quality - better than ever before: After a decade of improvement, asset quality in India's banking sector is superior to that of other leading Asian economies such as China, Malaysia and Indonesia. Three years ago, Indian banks were using treasury gains to provide for non-performing assets (NPAs) or write them off; today, however, recoveries are the single most significant route for NPA reduction. CRISIL's simulation of a stressed economic scenario reveals that, even if asset quality were to deteriorate significantly today, the impact on the banking sector would be manageable. This is primarily because of improved capital adequacy, greater diversity in asset portfolio, stronger credit profile of borrowers, and increased risk awareness among banks.
- Banking system adequately capitalised even under Basel-II Framework: CRISIL believes that the incremental capital requirement for the banking sector on the implementation of Basel II norms, and the demands from unprovided-for 'weak assets' are manageable on a systemic basis; 'weak assets' indicate assets that are of an inherently poor credit profile (including speculative exposures, current NPAs and delinquent accounts in case of retail portfolios).

Banks have raised around Rs.150 billion of capital in 2005-06 to finance the high credit growth and ready themselves for Basel II norms. The flexibility given to banks to raise different forms of capital, permitting the issue of hybrid capital, will help them maintain adequate capital levels on a systemic basis.

- Northbound rates not to hit banks' core profitability: CRISIL expects the core profitability of the banking sector to remain stable despite the increase in cost of funds. The banking sector has had a largely stable interest spread, between 2.6 and 3.2 per cent, for more than ten years (even in the increasing interest rate scenario in 1994-96). In 2005-06, there was a decline in the banking sector's core profitability (which excludes non-core aspects such as profits and losses on the investment book).

This was reflected in a lower Net Profitability Margin {NPM which is defined as (Yield on funds deployed) - (Average borrowing costs) - (Operating expense ratio) + (Fee income levels)}.

CRISIL believes the decline in profitability was temporary, as yields on a stock basis are expected to increase from 2006-07, aiding core profitability. CRISIL expects the banking sector's core profitability levels to remain range-bound, with net profitability margins of over 1.50 per cent over the medium term, and loan book expansion being the key driver determining overall profit levels.

STRENGTHENING INDIAN BANKING AND FINANCE: PROGRESS AND PROSPECTS

"We need greater productivity and efficiency to achieve the targets we set for ourselves, whether it be the macro-economic target of achieving 8 per cent growth in the Tenth Plan period or making our banking system strong and efficient and on par with international banks", this was the central message of the inaugural address of Dr. Bimal Jalan, Governor, Reserve Bank of India at the twenty-fourth Bank Economists' Conference.

The Conference was held between December 27 and 29 in Bangalore.

Plan Target not Difficult to Achieve

Referring to the targets set by the Tenth Plan of 8 per cent growth, poverty alleviation and improvement in human development indicator and the cynicism expressed about their achievement, Dr. Jalan unequivocally said, "I believe that the overall macro-economic situation has seldom been better in achieving the targets set by the Tenth Plan. Th e conditions cannot be more appropriate to meet the challenges in both the banking and the real sectors."

Contending that the growth target of 8 per cent envisaged by the Tenth Plan document was not at all difficult to achieve, the Governor pointed out that India had never faced a more favourable situation than it was at present. The Governor said that the conditions were right despite many adverse external factors.

The inflation was low, for instance, despite the most severe drought in the country; India's foreign exchange reserves were at the highest and healthiest level despite a hike in the oil prices, border tensions, global slowdown and tensions prevailing on the Iraq front.

In fact, the reserves were also healthy as they were not built up by increasing external debt, he pointed out. The Indian economy was also nudging towards 5-5.5 per cent growth despite lower agriculture production, slow industrial recovery and a global downturn. There was abundance of liquidity and the interest rates at long and short maturities were the lowest ever despite a high fiscal deficit and a high borrowing requirement of the government. In other words, if domestic and external resources could be a constraint in achieving growth targets, India faced none and therefore the environment was most conducive for growth, he pointed out.

To underscore the positive factors, the Governor recalled the earlier times when the presence of any of the constraints, such as, drought or higher oil prices, would have caused India to face tight liquidity, higher interest rates, high fiscal deficit, scarce foreign exchange and higher exchange controls.

"But today we face none of these and there is no difference of opinion that we are in the best possible situation to achieve the targeted growth", he stated unequivocally.

Increase Productivity and Reduce Costs

The answer to the cynicism despite many favourable conditions lied in low productivity, the Governor said and added that "For every rupee of capital spent by the government or by the private sector, we produce less," he stated. He added that inefficiency in the use of resources, tolerance of waste and slothfulness contributed to low productivity.

"Our savings rate is the highest but our rate of growth is low. Our cost of doing business is relatively high and returns are not commensurate with investments made" the Governor said and added that this was true also of the banking sector which suffers from high cost and low productivity as reflected in high spreads.

The important challenge of managing transformation would, for the banking sector, mean moving from high cost, low productivity and high spread to being more efficient, productive and competitive.

For this, the banks need to address four main areas viz., corporate governance, economic value added, technology upgradation and H RD. Of these, HRD is the more difficult area to tackle. In public sector institutions, there are more challenges to face.

"Taking examination to get into the system is the biggest challenge but once you get in there is no challenge" he observed. Increasing productivity and lowering cost per unit of output were the two biggest challenges faced by India, more specifically the banking and the financial system.

Keep Depositors' Trust

In addition to low productivity, the Governor dwelt upon the other two issues, namely prudential norms and supervision and regulation. He commended the progress made by India's banking and financial system in prudential norms and added that India was contributing at the conceptual level in the international forum and was in fact the chairperson of the committee contributing to the thinking on adoption of BASEL II norms in emerging economies.

Apart from these, India had also made signif icant progress on transparency, capital adequacy and disclosures. While the achievements were significant, India lagged behind in management of non-performing assets.

He stated that there were two reasons why the banking system should follow international norms. One, concern for depositors' money and second to face international competition.

The Governor pointed out that banking was the only institution that invested other people's money. On capital of 10 rupees they can lend 100 rupees. Bankers must be conscious of this and follow prudential norms of the highest order so that the public money is not threatened. "Banking system's edifice is based on trust, and that should not be eroded" he stressed.

At the international level, the non-adherence to globally accepted prudential norms would result in the international system doubting the repaying capacity of the Indian banks and make them uncompetitive in the international market. The Governor pointed out that no international forum would grudge the time table a country sets out to achieve the global standards.

He added that India was fruitfully participating in all international discussions on these issues and was evolving a framework for consultative process among the emerging economy.

Need for Greater Accountability

The Governor further stated that there are two different trends in area of supervision and regulation. Both, greater stress on supervision and regulation of the banking system and deregulation of financial markets with openness and transparency existed side by side. He also said that two economic factors were special to banking and financial system.

Unlike real sector, the impact of failure in a bank or financial unit has a more pervading effect. When an externality affects a banking unit, the depositors, borrowers and markets feel the impact immedi ately. Secondly, when something goes wrong, the only way to handle this is to take prompt corrective action. Deterioration in a bank or a financial unit does not have a linear course but has multiplying effect. This exponential effect is not seen in the real sector.

This situation can be tackled only by taking prompt corrective action. He said that in India, however, action is often postponed in the name of "doing good". Regulation is weak in some part of bank sector and prompt corrective action lukewarm.

This needs to be corrected by strengthening the legal framework and removing multiple levels of control and specifying a clear-cut supervisory authority. Depoliticisation of bank and bank's accountability of the depositors should be clearly emphasised.

THE CHANGING FACE OF BANKING

THE Indian financial sector is undergoing rapid change. Structural reforms aimed at improving the productivity and efficiency of the economy are apace.

The $28-billion sector, growing at roughly 15 per cent, has displayed remarkable stability over the years even when other markets in the Asian region were facing a crisis. The Indian financial sector has kept pace with the growing needs of its borrowers.

Changing Environment

The most important factor shaping today's world is globalisation. Companies are constantly in search of low-cost markets.

Technology is driving growth in production and productivity and competition is stiff. Secondly, rapid development in communication technology has lead to greater integration of global financial markets, in turn boosting private capital flows and foreign direct investment.

A third factor is the increasing share of emerging market economies in world trade. Another fallout of globalisation is the increase in volatility and vulnerability of markets. This calls for the adoption of international standards and global benchmarks.

Aligning with Global Standards

To strengthen India's banking system in an increasingly competitive environment and guard against financial fragility, financial sector reforms were initiated as part of the economic reforms launched in the country since 1991-92. Significant progress has been made in the past few years to bring the Indian Banking system closer to international standards.

India has adopted international prudential norms and practices with regard to capital adequacy, income recognition, provisioning requirement and supervision and these norms have been progressively tightened over the years.

There has been a steady decline in the level of resource pre-emption from the banking system in the form of CRR (cash reserve ratio) and SLR (statutory liquidity ratio). Interest rates in various segments of financial markets have been deregulated in a phased manner.

The mark-to-market practice for valuation of government securities has been gradually enhanced and further refinement, in line with international best practices, carried out in valuation and classification of investment by banks.

Risk management in banks has been strengthened and measures put in place to mitigate credit and market risks and efforts are on to measure and control operational risk. Banks have been given greater freedom in investing as also raising funds abroad and managing their external liability, subject to prudential guidelines.

In the area of supervision, the Basel core principles for effective banking supervision are being followed. Along with off-site surveillance there is periodic on-site monitoring of the risk profile of banks and their compliance with prudential guidelines and a "CAMELS"-based rating system is being followed. The Reserve Bank of India's regulatory and supervisory responsibility has been widened to include banking institutions and non-banking financial companies.

The end result, is that the Indian banking sector has been considerably strengthened; there is greater transparency and closer convergence of Indian financial system with practices prevailing in international financial markets.

There is special focus on corporate governance and the setting up of specialised board-level panels such as the executive, risk management, audit, compensation, asset-liability management committees, and so on.

The RBI's Standing Committee on International Financial Standards and Codes under the Chairmanship of Dr Y. V. Reddy has identified global standards and codes as part of the efforts to create a sound financial architecture aligned with global practices.

Moving Forward

But there are some areas that need greater attention.

Need to check NPAs: The biggest challenge is the problem of NPAs (non-performing assets). Around 12 per cent of bank credit is locked in NPAs, which means that banks do not earn any interest on NPA accounts. This is a drain on the financial health of banks. If banks have to cut their costs and improve performance, they must reduce their NPAs. The Government has re-promulgated the ordinance to help banks expedite recovery. This calls for strengthening credit appraisal and risk management and developing review and control systems in tune with the changing requirements.

Strengthening internal controls: While the information technology explosion has been beneficial, it has also brought with it some unsavoury side-effects.The increase in frauds and scams in the financial sector is a cause for concern and calls for the strengthening of internal controls of banks and financial institutions.

Focus on Indian economy: Even as banks move closer to international standards, they cannot lose touch with the realities of the Indian economy. In this context, agriculture, small industries/businesses and the services sectors, must be given special consideration and credit flow to the rural sector increased. In an age where the world has become smaller and money moves as quickly as information, achieving global benchmarks is important for global players.

But underlying this is the need to have sound fundamentals. There is no doubt that only banks and financial institutions that are focussed on efficiency, productivity and profitability have a chance to survive in a highly competitive environment and therefore need to equip themselves thoroughly to face the future competition.

THE TRENDS IN INDIAN BANKING

The Indian banking can be broadly categorized into nationalized (government owned), private banks and specialized banking institutions.The Reserve Bank of India acts a centralized body monitoring any discrepancies and shortcoming in the system. Since the nationalization of banks in 1969, the public sector banks or the nationalized banks have acquired a place of prominence and has since then seen tremendous progress.

The need to become highly customer focused has forced the slow-moving public sector banks to adopt a fast track approach. The unleashing of products and services through the net has galvanized players at all levels of the banking and financial institutions market grid to look anew at their existing portfolio offering.

Conservative banking practices allowed Indian banks to be insulated partially from the Asian currency crisis.Indian banks are now quoting al higher valuation when compared to banks in other Asian countries (viz. Hong Kong, Singapore, Philippines etc.) that have major problems linked to huge Non Performing Assets (NPAs) and payment defaults. Co-operative banks are nimble footed in approach and armed with efficient branch networks focus primarily on the 'high revenue' niche retail segments.

The Indian banking has finally worked up to the competitive dynamics of the 'new' Indian market and is addressing the relevant issues to take on the multifarious challenges of globalization. Banks that employ IT solutions are perceived to be 'futuristic' and proactive players capable of mèeting the multifarious requirements of the large customers base. Private banks have been fast on the uptake and are reorienting their strategies using the internet as a medium The Internet has emerged as the new and challenging frontier of marketing with the conventional physical world tenets being just as applicable like in any other marketing medium.

The Indian banking has come from a long way from being a sleepy business institution to a highly proactive and dynamic entity. This transformation has been largely brought about by the large dose of liberalization and economic reforms that allowed banks to explore new business opportunities rather than generating revenues from conventional streams (i.e. borrowing and lending).

The banking in India is highly fragmented with 30 banking units contributing to almost 50% of deposits and 60% of advances. Indian nationalized banks (banks owned by the government) continue to be the major lenders in the economy due to their sheer size and penetrative networks which assures them high deposit mobilization. The Indian banking can be broadly categorized into nationalized, private banks and specialized banking institutions.

The Reserve Bank of India act as a centralized body monitoring any discrepancies and shortcoming in the system. It is the foremost monitoring body in the Indian financial sector. The nationalized banks (i.e. government-owned banks) continue to dominate the Indian banking arena. Industry estimates indicate that out of 274 commercial banks operating in India, 223 banks are in the public sector and 51 are in the private sector.

The private sector bank grid also includes 24 foreign banks that have started their operations here. Under the ambit of the nationalized banks come the specialized banking institutions. These co-operatives, rural banks focus on areas of agriculture, rural development etc.

BANKING ON RETAIL

With a jump in the Indian economy from a manufacturing sector, that never really took off, to a nascent service sector, Banking as a whole is undergoing a change. A larger option for the consumer is getting translated into a larger demand for financial products and customisation of services is fast becoming the norm than a competitive advantage.

With the Retail banking sector expected to grow at a rate of 30% [Chanda Kochhar, ED, ICICI Bank] players are focussing more and more on the Retail and are waking up to the potential of this sector of banking.

At the same time, the banking sector as a whole is seeing structural changes in regulatory frameworks and securitisation and stringent NPA norms expected to be in place by 2004 means the faster one adapts to these changing dynamics, the faster is one expected to gain the advantage.

Potential for Retail in India: Is Sky the Limit?

The Indian players are bullish on the Retail business and this is not totally unfounded. There are two main reasons behind this. Firstly, it is now undeniable that the face of the Indian consumer is changing. This is reflected in a change in the urban household income pattern. The direct fallout of such a change will be the consumption patterns and hence the banking habits of Indians, which will now be skewed towards Retail products. At the same time, India compares pretty poorly with the other economies of the world that are now becoming comparable in terms of spending patterns with the opening up of our economy. For instance, while the total outstanding Retail loans in Taiwan is around 41% of GDP, the figure in India stands at less than 5%.

The comparison with the West is even more staggering. Another comparison that is natural when comparing Retail sectors is the use of credit cards. Here also, the potential lies in the fact that of all the consumer expenditure in India in 2001, less than 1% was through plastic, the corresponding US figure standing at 18%.

But how Competitive are the Players?

The fact that the statistics reveal a huge potential also brings with it a threat that is true for any sector of a country that is opening up. Just how competitive are our banks? Is the threat of getting drubbed by foreign competition real? To analyze this, one needs to get into the shoes of the foreign banks. In other words, how do they see us? Are we good takeover targets?

Going by international standards, a large portion of the Indian population is simply not "bankable" - taking ·.rofitability into consideration.

On the other hand, the financial services market is highly over-leveraged in India. Competition is fierce, particularly from local private banks such as HDFC and ICICI, in the business of home, car and consumer loans. There, precisely lie the pitfalls of such explosive growth. All banks are targeting the fluffiest segment i.e. the upwardly mobile urban salaried class. Although the players are spreading their operations into segments like self- employed and the semi-urban rich, it is an open secret that the big city Indian yuppies form the most profitable segment. Over-dependence on this segment is bound to bring in inflexibility in the business.

What about the Foreign Giants?

The foreign banks have identified this problem but there are certain systematic risks involved in operating in the Retail market for them.

These include regulatory restrictions that prevent them from expanding their branch network. So these banks often take the Direct Selling Agent (DSA) route whereby low-end jobs like sourcing or transaction processing are outsourced to small regional layers. So now on, when you see a loan mela or a road show showcasing the retail bouquet of an elite MNC giant, you know that a significant commission earned out of any such booking gets ploughed back to our own economy. Perhaps, one of the biggest impediments in foreign players leveraging the Indian markets is the absence of positive credit bureaus. In the west the risk profile can be easily mapped to things like SSNs and this information can be publicly traded.

So all for the Keeping Then?

This will perhaps be the most wrongful inference that can be drawn from the above. We just cannot afford to look inwards and repeat the mistakes that were the side effects of the Nationalization of the Banking System. A growing market can never be an alibi for lack of innovation. Indian banks have shown little or no interest in innovative tailor-made products.

They have often tried to copy process designs that have been tested, albeit successfully, in the West. Each economic culture has its own traits and one who successfully adapts those to the business is the eventual winner. A case in point is the successful implementation of micro-credit networks in Bangladesh. Positioning a bank as a tech-savvy financial vendor in a country where Internet penetration is an abysmal 1.65% can only add to the over-leveraging as pointed out earlier.

The focus of the sector should remain in macroeconomic wealth creation and not increasing the per capita indebtedness that will do little but add to the NPA burden. Retail Banking in India has to be developed in the Indian way, notwithstanding the long queues in front of the teller counters in the Public sector banks!

7

History of Banking in India

INTRODUCTION

The government's regular policy for Indian bank since 1969 has paid rich dividends with the nationalisation of 14 major private banks of India. Not long ago, an account holder had to wait for hours at the bank counters for getting a draft or for withdrawing his own money. Today, he has a choice. Gone are days when the most efficient bank transferred money from one branch to other in two days. Now it is simple as instant messaging or dial a pizza. Money have become the order of the day.Without a sound and effective banking system in India it cannot have a healthy economy. The banking system of India should not only be hassle free but it should be able to meet new challenges posed by the technology and any other external and internal factors.

For the past three decades India's banking system has several outstanding achievements to its credit. The most striking is its extensive reach. It is no longer confined to only metropolitans or cosmopolitans in India. In fact, Indian banking system has reached even to the remote corners of the country. This is one of the main reason of India's growth process.

The first bank in India, though conservative, was established in 1786. From 1786 till today, the journey of Indian Banking System can be segregated into three distinct phases. They are as mentioned below:

- Early phase from 1786 to 1969 of Indian Banks
- Nationalisation of Indian Banks and up to 1991 prior to Indian banking sector Reforms.
- New phase of Indian Banking System with the advent of Indian Financial & Banking Sector Reforms after 1991.

To make this write-up more explanatory, I prefix the scenario as Phase I, Phase II and Phase III.

BANKS IN INDIA

In India the banks are being segregated in different groups. Each group has their own benefits and limitations in operating in India. Each has their own dedicated target market. Few of them only work in rural sector while others in both rural as well as urban. Many even are only catering in cities. Some are of Indian origin and some are foreign players.

All these details and many more is discussed over here. The banks and its relation with the customers, their mode of operation, the names of banks under different groups and other such useful informations are talked about.

One more section has been taken note of is the upcoming foreign banks in India. The RBI has shown certain interest to involve more of foreign banks than the existing one recently. This step has paved a way for few more foreign banks to start business in India.

Major Banks in India

- ABN-AMRO Bank
- Abu Dhabi Commercial Bank
- American Express Bank
- Andhra Bank

- Allahabad Bank
- Axis Bank (Earlier UTI Bank)
- Bank of Baroda
- Bank of India
- Bank of Maharastra
- Bank of Punjab
- Bank of Rajasthan
- Bank of Ceylon
- BNP Paribas Bank
- Canara Bank
- Catholic Syrian Bank
- Central Bank of India
- Centurion Bank
- China Trust Commercial Bank
- Citi Bank
- City Union Bank
- Corporation Bank
- Dena Bank
- Deutsche Bank
- Development Credit Bank
- Dhanalakshmi Bank
- Federal Bank
- HDFC Bank
- HSBC
- ICICI Bank
- IDBI Bank
- Indian Bank

- Indian Overseas Bank
- IndusInd Bank
- ING Vysya Bank
- Jammu & Kashmir Bank
- JPMorgan Chase Bank
- Karnataka Bank
- Karur Vysya Bank
- Laxmi Vilas Bank
- Oriental Bank of Commerce
- Punjab National Bank
- Punjab & Sind Bank
- Scotia Bank
- South Indian Bank
- Standard Chartered Bank
- State Bank of India (SBI)
- State Bank of Bikaner & Jaipur
- State Bank of Hyderabad
- State Bank of Indore
- State Bank of Mysore
- State Bank of Saurastra
- State Bank of Travancore
- Syndicate Bank
- Taib Bank
- UCO Bank
- Union Bank of India
- United Bank of India
- United Bank Of India

- United Western Bank
- Vijaya Bank

PUBLIC SECTOR BANKS IN INDIA

Among the Public Sector Banks in India, United Bank of India is one of the 14 major banks which were nationalised on July 19, 1969. Its predecessor, in the Public Sector Banks, the United Bank of India Ltd., was formed in 1950 with the amalgamation of four banks viz. Comilla Banking Corporation Ltd. (1914), Bengal Central Bank Ltd. (1918), Comilla Union Bank Ltd. (1922) and Hooghly Bank Ltd. (1932).

Oriental Bank of Commerce (OBC), a Governmet of India Undertaking offers Domestic, NRI and Commercial banking services. OBC is implementing a GRAMEEN PROJECT in Dehradun District (UP) and Hanumangarh District (Raiasthan) disbursing small loans. This Public Secotor Bank India has implemented 14 point action plan for strengthening of credit delivery to women and has designated 5 branches as specialized branches for women entrepreneurs.

The following are the list of Public Sector Banks in India

- Allahabad Bank
- Andhra Bank
- Bank of Baroda
- Bank of India
- Bank of Maharastra
- Canara Bank
- Central Bank of India
- Corporation Bank
- Dena Bank
- Indian Bank
- Indian Overseas Bank

- Oriental Bank of Commerce
- Punjab & Sind Bank
- Punjab National Bank
- Syndicate Bank
- UCO Bank
- Union Bank of India
- United Bank of India
- Vijaya Bank

List of State Bank of India and its subsidiary, a Public Sector Banks

- State Bank of India
  - — State Bank of Bikaner & Jaipur
  - — State Bank of Hyderabad
  - — State Bank of Indore
  - — State Bank of Mysore
  - — State Bank of Saurastra
  - — State Bank of Travancore.

Phase I

The General Bank of India was set up in the year 1786. Next came Bank of Hindustan and Bengal Bank. The East India Company established Bank of Bengal (1809), Bank of Bombay (1840) and Bank of Madras (1843) as independent units and called it Presidency Banks. These three banks were amalgamated in 1920 and Imperial Bank of India was established which started as private shareholders banks, mostly Europeans shareholders.

In 1865 Allahabad Bank was established and first time exclusively by Indians, Punjab National Bank Ltd. was set up in 1894 with headquarters at Lahore. Between 1906 and 1913,

Bank of India, Central Bank of India, Bank of Baroda, Canara Bank, Indian Bank, and Bank of Mysore were set up. Reserve Bank of India came in 1935.

During the first phase the growth was very slow and banks also experienced periodic failures between 1913 and 1948. There were approximately 1100 banks, mostly small. To streamline the functioning and activities of commercial banks, the Government of India came up with The Banking Companies Act, 1949 which was later changed to Banking Regulation Act 1949 as per amending Act of 1965 (Act No. 23 of 1965). Reserve Bank of India was vested with extensive powers for the supervision of banking in india as the Central Banking Authority.

During those days public has lesser confidence in the banks. As an aftermath deposit mobilisation was slow. Abreast of it the savings bank facility provided by the Postal department was comparatively safer. Moreover, funds were largely given to traders.

Phase II

Government took major steps in this Indian Banking Sector Reform after independence. In 1955, it nationalised Imperial Bank of India with extensive banking facilities on a large scale specially in rural and semi-urban areas.

It formed State Bank of india to act as the principal agent of RBI and to handle banking transactions of the Union and State Governments all over the country.

Seven banks forming subsidiary of State Bank of India was nationalised in 1960 on 19th July, 1969, major process of nationalisation was carried out. It was the effort of the then Prime Minister of India, Mrs. Indira Gandhi. 14 major commercial banks in the country was nationalised.

Second phase of nationalisation Indian Banking Sector Reform was carried out in 1980 with seven more banks. This step brought 80% of the banking segment in India under Government ownership.

The following are the steps taken by the Government of India to Regulate Banking Institutions in the Country:

- 1949 : Enactment of Banking Regulation Act.
- 1955 : Nationalisation of State Bank of India.
- 1959 : Nationalisation of SBI subsidiaries.
- 1961 : Insurance cover extended to deposits.
- 1969 : Nationalisation of 14 major banks.
- 1971 : Creation of credit guarantee corporation.
- 1975 : Creation of regional rural banks.
- 1980 : Nationalisation of seven banks with deposits over 200 crore.

After the nationalisation of banks, the branches of the public sector bank India rose to approximately 800% in deposits and advances took a huge jump by 11,000%.

Banking in the sunshine of Government ownership gave the public implicit faith and immense confidence about the sustainability of these institutions.

Phase III

This phase has introduced many more products and facilities in the banking sector in its reforms measure. In 1991, under the chairmanship of M Narasimham, a committee was set up by his name which worked for the liberalisation of banking practices.

The country is flooded with foreign banks and their ATM stations. Efforts are being put to give a satisfactory service to customers. Phone banking and net banking is introduced. The entire system became more convenient and swift. Time is given more importance than money.

The financial system of India has shown a great deal of resilience. It is sheltered from any crisis triggered by any external macroeconomics shock as other East Asian Countries suffered.

This is all due to a flexible exchange rate regime, the foreign reserves are high, the capital account is not yet fully convertible, and banks and their customers have limited foreign exchange exposure

PRIVATE SECTOR BANKS IN INDIA

Private banking in India was practiced since the begining of banking system in India. The first private bank in India to be set up in Private Sector Banks in India was IndusInd Bank. It is one of the fastest growing Bank Private Sector Banks in India. IDBI ranks the tength largest development bank in the world as Private Banks in India and has promoted a world class institutions in India.

The first Private Bank in India to receive an in principle approval from the Reserve Bank of India was Housing Development Finance Corporation Limited, to set up a bank in the private sector banks in India as part of the RBI's liberalisation of the Indian Banking Industry. It was incorporated in August 1994 as HDFC Bank Limited with registered office in Mumbai and commenced operations as Scheduled Commercial Bank in January 1995.

ING Vysya, yet another Private Bank of India was incorporated in the year 1930. Bangalore has a pride of place for having the first branch inception in the year 1934. With successive years of patronage and constantly setting new standards in banking, ING Vysya Bank has many credits to its account.

List of Private Banks in India

- Bank of Punjab
- Bank of Rajasthan

- Catholic Syrian Bank
- Centurion Bank
- City Union Bank
- Dhanalakshmi Bank
- Development Credit Bank
- Federal Bank
- HDFC Bank
- ICICI Bank
- IDBI Bank
- IndusInd Bank
- ING Vysya Bank
- Jammu & Kashmir Bank
- Karnataka Bank
- Karur Vysya Bank
- Laxmi Vilas Bank
- South Indian Bank
- United Western Bank
- UTI Bank

Co-Operative Banks In India

The Co operative banks in India started functioning almost 100 years ago. The Cooperative bank is an important constituent of the Indian Financial System, judging by the role assigned to co operative, the expectations the co operative is supposed to fulfil, their number, and the number of offices the cooperative bank operate.

Though the co operative movement originated in the West, but the importance of such banks have assumed in India is rarely paralleled anywhere else in the world. The cooperative banks in India plays an important role even today in rural financing.

The businessess of cooperative bank in the urban areas also has increased phenomenally in recent years due to the sharp increase in the number of primary co-operative banks.

Co operative Banks in India are registered under the Co-operative Societies Act. The cooperative bank is also regulated by the RBI. They are governed by the Banking Regulations Act 1949 and Banking Laws (Co-operative Societies) Act, 1965.

Cooperative banks in India finance rural areas under:

- Farming
- Cattle
- Milk
- Hatchery
- Personal finance

Cooperative banks in India finance urban areas under:

- Self-employment
- Industries
- Small scale units
- Home finance
- Consumer finance
- Personal finance

Some Facts about Cooperative Banks in India

- Some cooperative banks in India are more forward than many of the state and private sector banks.
- According to NAFCUB the total deposits & lendings of Cooperative Banks in India is much more than Old Private Sector Banks & also the New Private Sector Banks.
- This exponential growth of Co operative Banks in India is attributed mainly to their much better local reach, personal interaction with customers, their ability to catch the nerve of the local clientele.

8

Regulation of Banking and Its Supervision

INTRODUCTION

In certain areas, as for instance, in the urban cooperative banking segment, the regulatory requirements leave considerable scope for regulatory arbitrage and even circumvention. The problem is rendered more complex by the existence of regulatory overlap between the Central Government, the State Governments and the Reserve Bank. Regulatory overlap has impeded the speed of regulatory response to emerging problems. The need for removing multiple regulatory jurisdiction over the cooperative banking sector has been reiterated on several occasions.

In this regard, the Reserve Bank has proposed the setting up of an apex supervisory body for urban cooperative banks under the control of a high-level supervisory board consisting of representatives of the Central governments, the State governments, the Reserve Bank and experts. The apex body is expected to ensure compliance with prudential requirements and also supervise on-site inspections and off-site surveillance. Recent developments in certain segments of the financial sector have also brought to the fore issues relating to corporate governance in banks. As part of on-going reforms, boards have been given greater autonomy to prescribe internal control guidelines, risk management and procedures for market discipline and accountability. It is extremely important that greater vigilance over adherence to these norms goes hand-in-hand with greater autonomy. Recent evidence of transgression of prudential guidelines by a few banks has raised the issue of the audit and supervisory functions of boards. As we move towards a more deregulated financial regime, these functions have to be transferred from either the Government or the Reserve Bank to bank boards. This imposes a greater responsibility and accountability on the bank management. It is in this context that a consultative group of directors of select banks and other experts has been set up to recommend measures to strengthen the internal supervisory ro le of boards.

The objective is to obtain a feedback on how boards function vis-à-vis compliance with prudential norms, transparency and disclosure, functioning of the audit committee, etc., and to devise effective mechanisms for ensuring management discipline. Several other initiatives in improving the supervisory function have been undertaken, including a prudential supervisory reporting system for financial institutions, improvements in procedures for financial inspection, sensitising the general public for better regulation of the activities of NBFCs and enactment of appropriate legislation to protect depositor interests in some States. Major legal reforms have been initiated in areas such as security laws, the Negotiable Instruments Act, bank frauds and the regulatory framework of banking.

The Reserve Bank has also accepted the principle of transfer of ownership to the Government in respect of some financial institutions in view of the conflict of interest that may arise in the conduct of its supervisory function. It is expected that these initiatives will pave the way for an efficient, and risk-based supervisory environment in India. Progressive strengthening, deepening and refinement of the regulatory and supervisory system for the financial sector have been important elements of financial sector reforms. In the long run, it is the supervision and regulation function that is critical in safeguarding financial stability. There is also some evidence that proactive and effective supervision contributes to the efficiency of financial intermediation. Financial sector supervision is expected to become increasingly risk-based and concerned with validating systems rather than setting them. This will entail procedures for sound internal evaluation of risk for banks. As mentioned earlier, bank managements will have to develop internal capital assessment processes in accordance with their risk profile and control environment. These internal processes would then be subjected to review and supervisory intervention if necessary. The emphasis will be on evaluating the quality of risk management and the adequacy of risk conta inment. In such an environment, credibility assigned by markets to risk disclosures will hold only if they are validated by supervisors. Thus effective and appropriate supervision is critical for the effectiveness of capital requirements and market discipline.

TECHNOLOGY IN BANKING

Nobel Laureate Robert Solow had once remarked that computers are seen everywhere excepting in productivity statistics. More recent developments have shown how far this state of affairs has changed. Innovation in technology and worldwide revolution in information and communication technology (ICT) have emerged as dynamic sources of productivity growth. The relationship between IT and banking is fundamentally symbiotic. In the banking sector, IT can reduce costs, increase volumes, and facilitate customised products; similarly, IT requires banking and financial services to facilitate its growth. As far as the banking system is concerned, the payment system is perhaps the most important mechanism through which such interactive dynamics gets manifested.

Recognising the importance of payments and settlement systems in the economy, we have embarked on technology based solutions for the improvement of the payment and settlement system infrastructure, coupled with the introduction of new payment products such as the computerised settlement of clearing transactions, use of Magnetic Ink Character Recognition (MICR) technology for cheque clearing which currently accounts for 65 per cent of the value of cheques processed in the country, the computerisation of Government Accounts and Currency Chest transactions, operationalisation of Delivery versus Payment (DvP) for Government securities transactions. Two-way inter-city cheque collection and imaging have been operationalised at the four metros. The coverage of Electronic Clearing Service (Debit and Credit) has been significantly expanded to encourage non-paper based funds movement and develop the provision of a centralised facility for effecting payments. The scheme for Electronic Fu nds Transfer operated by the Reserve Bank has been significantly augmented and is now available across thirteen major cities. The scheme, which was originally intended for small value transactions, is processing high value (up to Rs.2 crore) from October 1, 2001. The Centralised Funds Management System (CFMS), which would enable banks to obtain consolidated account-wise and centre-wise positions of their balances with all 17 offices of the Deposits Accounts Departments of the Reserve Bank has begun to be implemented in a phased manner from November 2001.

A holistic approach has been adopted towards designing and development of a modern, robust, efficient, secure and integrated payment and settlement system taking into account certain aspects relating to potential risks, legal framework and the impact on the operational framework of monetary policy.

The approach to the modernisation of the payment and settlement system in India has been three-pronged: (a) consolidation, (b) development, and (c) integration. The consolidation of the existing payment systems revolves around strengthening Computerised Cheque clearing, expanding the reach of Electronic Clearing Services and Electronic Funds Transfer by providing for systems with the latest levels of technology.

The critical elements in the developmental strategy are the opening of new clearing houses, interconnection of clearing houses through the INFINET; optimising the deployment of resources by banks through Real Time Gross Settlement System, Centralised Funds Management System (CFMS); Nego tiated Dealing System (NDS) and the Structured Financial Messaging Solution (SFMS). While integration of the various payment products with the systems of individual banks is the thrust area, it requires a high degree of standardisation within a bank and seamless interfaces across banks.

The setting up of the apex-level National Payments Council in May 1999 and the operationalisation of the INFINET by the Institute for Development and Research in Banking Technology (IDRBT), Hyderabad have been some important developments in the direction of providing a communication network for the exclusive use of banks and financial institutions.

Membership in the INFINET has been opened up to all banks in addition to those in the public sector. At the base of all inter-bank message transfers using the INFINET is the Structured Financial Messaging System (SFMS). It would serve as a secure communication carrier with templates for intra- and inter-bank messages in fixed message formats that will facilitate 'straight through processing'. All inter-bank transactions would be stored and switched at the central hub at Hyderabad while intra-bank messages will be switched and stored by the bank gateway. Security features of the SFMS would match international standards.

In order to maximise the benefits of such efforts, banks have to take pro-active measures to :

- further strengthen their infrastructure in respect of standardisation, high levels of security and communication and networking;
- achieve inter-branch connectivity early;

- popularise the usage of the scheme of electronic funds transfer (EFT); and
- institute arrangements for an RTGS environment online with a view to integrating into a secure and consolidated payment system.

Information technology has immense untapped potential in banking. Strengthening of information technology in banks could improve the effectiveness of asset-liability management in banks. Building up of a related data-base on a real time basis would enhance the forecasting of liquidity greatly even at the branch level. This could contribute to enhancing the risk management capabilities of banks.

HUMAN RESOURCE DEVELOPMENT IN BANKING

A recurring theme in the annual BECON Conference has been the need to focus on developing human resources to cope with the rapidly changing scenario. The core function of HRD in the banking industry is to facilitate performance improvement, measured not only in terms of financial indicators of operational efficiency but also in terms of the quality of financial services provided. Factors such as skills, attitudes and knowledge of personnel play a critical role in determining the competitiveness of the financial sector. The quality of human resources indicates the ability of banks to deliver value to customers. Capital and technology are replicable, but not human capital which needs to be viewed as a valuable resource for the achievement of competitive advantage. The primary emphasis needs to be on integrating human resource management (HRM) strategies with the business strategy. HRM strategies include managing change, creating commitment, achieving flexibility and improving t eamwork. These processes underlie the complementary processes that represent the overt aspects of HRM, such as recruitment, placement, performance management, reward management, and employee relations. A forward looking approach would involve moving towards self-assessment of competency and developmental needs as a part of a continuous learning cycle.

The Indian banking industry has been an important driving force behind the nation's economic development. The emerging environment poses both opportunities and threats, in particular, to the public sector banks. How well these are met will mainly depend on the extent to which the banks leverage their primary assets i.e., human resources in the context of the changing economic and business environment. It is obvious that the public sector banks' hierarchical structure, which gives preference to seniority over performance, is not the best environment for attracting the best talent from among the young in a competitive environment. A radical transformation of the existing personnel structure in public sector banks is unlikely to be practical, at least in the foreseeable future. However, certain improvements can be made in the recruitment practices as well as in on-the-job training and redeployment of those who are already employed. There are several institutions in the country which cat er exclusively to the needs of human resource development in the banking industry. It is worthwhile to consider broad-basing the courses conducted in these institutions among other higher-level educational institutions so that specialisation in the area of banking and financial services becomes an option in higher education curriculums. In the area of information technology, Indian professionals are world leaders and building synergies between the IT and banking industries will sharpen the competitive edge of our banks.

The changing environment, the forces of globalisation and liberalisation and the advances in information and communication technology have major HR implications for the Reserve Bank as well. Financial products are becoming increasingly complex and diverse, while the markets in which they trade get progressively deregulated. The need to adopt global best practices in financial sector regulation and supervision, and adapt them to the domestic environment, places a premium on the skills and expertise of the Bank's human resources. Again, the functioning and policies of public institutions, such as the Reserve Bank, are increasingly subject to public discussion and debate. This calls for greater transparency, more effective communication, and a high degree of professionalism in the Bank's staff. This warrants continuous upgradation of human resource management strategies with a view to enhancing the level of knowledge, sharpening skills and also to instill the necessary attitudes and work cultu re. The Reserve Bank is now devoting considerable attention to these areas at the entry level as well as at different levels of career development of its staff.

THE ROLE OF ECONOMISTS

In my inaugural address to BECON, 2000 I had discussed the crucial role of bank economists in transforming the banking system in India. Economists have to be more 'mainstreamed' within the operational structure of commercial banks. Apart from the traditional functioning of macro-scanning, the inter-linkages between treasuries, dealing rooms and trading rooms of banks need to be viewed not only with the day-to-day needs of operational necessity, but also with analytical content and policy foresight.

Today, operational aspects of the functioning of banks are attracting intensive research by professional economists. In particular, measuring and modeling different kinds of risks faced by banks, the behaviour of risk-return relationships associated with different portfolio mixes and the impact of fluctuations in financial markets on the financial performance of banks are areas which lend themselves to analytical and empirical appraisal by economists and econometricians.

They, in turn, are discovering the degrees of freedom and room for analytical maneuver in high frequency information generated by the day-to-day functioning of banks. It is vital that we develop an environment where these synergies are nurtured so as to serve the longer-term strategic interests of banks. Even in real time trading and portfolio decisions, the fundamental analysis of economists provides an independent assessment of market behaviour, reinforcing technical analysis.

A serious limitation of the applicability of standard economic analysis to banking relates to the inadequacies of the data-base.

Absence of long time series data storage in the banking industry often poses serious problems to the quest for the formal analytical relationships between variables. Even if such data exist, the presence of structural breaks may blur meaningful analysis based on traditional formulation. Economists need to think innovatively to overcome this problem.

Use of panel regression, non-parametric methods and multivariate analyses could go a long way in understanding and validating behaviourial relationships in banking.

Another important challenge for the economics profession is to develop proper models for measurement of various risks in Indian conditions. This is a necessity in view of the move towards risk-based supervision.

Quantification of operational risks and calibration of Value at Risk (VaR) models pose major computational challenge to bankers and policy makers alike, particularly in India.

A major difficulty lies in identifying the right statistical model that determines the underlying distribution suited to the particular category of operational loss, and building the necessary database for deriving operationally meaningful conclusions.

In my inaugural address last year, I had also emphasised the need for bank economists to come out of their narrow specialisation and address operational issues relating to banking and finance.

In order to make a meaningful contribution to banking, economists must have the experience of working in operational areas of banks.

For this purpose, economists need to 'soil their hands' in dealing rooms, treasuries and investment units, credit authorisation and loan recovery, strategic management groups and management information systems of the banks to understand the ground realities.

There are also 'economies' to be gained from field-level credit appraisal, asset recovery, debt restructuring, market and consumer behaviour in which banks are involved. Thus, the profession needs to amalgamate the objectivity and theoretical soundness of economics with the functional dimensions of banking and finance.

It is this combination of specialist training with operational experience, which is going to make t he economics profession relevant to the changing face of banking in India.

Universal Banking

Since the early 1990s, banking systems worldwide have been going through a rapid transformation. Mergers, amalgamations and acquisitions have been undertaken on a large scale in order to gain size and to focus more sharply on competitive strengths. This consolidation has produced financial conglomerates that are expected to maximise economies of scale and scope by 'bundling' the production of financial services. The general trend has been towards downstream universal banking where banks have undertaken traditionally non-banking activities such as investment banking, insurance, mortgage financing, securitisation, and particularly, insurance. Upstream linkages, where non-banks undertake banking business, are also on the increase. The global experience can be segregated into broadly three models. There is the Swedish or Hong Kong type model in which the banking corporate engages in in-house activities associated with banking. In Germany and the UK, certain types of activities are requi red to be carried out by separate subsidiaries. In the US type model, there is a holding company structure and separately capitalised subsidiaries.

In India, the first impulses for a more diversified financial intermediation were witnessed in the 1980s and 1990s when banks were allowed to undertake leasing, investment banking, mutual funds, factoring, hire-purchase activities through separate subsidiaries. By the mid-1990s, all restrictions on project financing were removed and banks were allowed to undertake several activities in-house. In the recent period, the focus is on Development Financial Institutions (DFIs), which have been allowed to set up banking subsidiaries and to enter the insurance business along with banks. DFIs were also allowed to undertake working capital financing and to raise short-term funds within limits. It was the Narasimham Committee II Report (1998) which suggested that the DFIs should convert themselves into banks or non-bank financial companies, and this conversion was endorsed by the Khan Working Group (1998). The Reserve Bank's Discussion Paper (1999) and the feedback thereon indicated the desirabili ty of universal banking from the point of view of efficiency of resource use, but it also emphasised the need to take into account factors such as the status of reforms, the state of preparedness of the institutions, and a viable transition path while moving in the desired direction.

Accordingly, the mid-term review of monetary and credit policy, October 1999 and the annual policy statements of April 2000 and April 2001 enunciated the broad approach to universal banking and the Reserve Bank's circular of April 2001 set out the operational and regulatory aspects of conversion of DFIs into universal banks. The need to proceed with planning and foresight is necessary for several reasons. The move towards universal banking would not provide a panacea for the endemic weaknesses of a DFI or its liquidity and solvency problems and/or operational difficulties arising from undercapitalisation, non-performing assets, and asset liability mismatches, etc. The overriding consideration should be the objectives and strategic interests of the financial institution concerned in the context of meeting the varied needs of customers, subject to normal prudential norms applicable to banks. From the point of view of the regulatory framework, the movement towards universal banking shou ld entrench stability of the financial system, preserve the safety of public deposits, improve efficiency in financial intermediation, ensure healthy competition, and impart transparent and equitable regulation.

CONCLUSION

There is greater awareness now of the need to prepare the banking system for the technical and capital requirements of the emerging prudential regime and a greater focus on core strengths and niche strategies. How close are we to the vision of a sound and well-functioning banking system that I outlined a year ago? It is fair to say that despite a turbulent year and many challenges, we have made some progress towards this goal.

There has been progressive intensification of financial sector reforms, and the financial sector as a whole is more sensitised than before to the need for internal strength and effective management as well as to the overall concerns for financial stability. At the same time, in view of greater disclosure and tougher prudential norms, the weaknesses in our financial system are more apparent than before. We have also made some progress in assessing our financial system against international best practices and in benchmarking the future directions of progress. Several contemplated changes in the surrounding legal and institutional environment have been proposed for legislation.

Nevertheless, several sources of vulnerability persist. The NPA levels remain too large by international standards and concerns relating to management and supervision within the ambit of corporate governance are being tested during the period of downturn of economic activity.

There is also a sense that we have a lot to acquire and adapt in terms of the technical expertise necessary to measure and manage risks better. The structure of the financial system is changing and supervisory and regulatory regimes are experiencing the strains of accommodating these changes. Certain weak links in the decentralised banking and non-bank financial sectors have also come to notice.

We should strive to move towards realising our vision of an efficient and sound banking system of international standards with redoubled vigour. Our greatest asset in this endeavour is the fund of technical and scientific human capital formation available in the country. The themes which are being covered in this Conference under structural, operational and governance issues should help in defining the road map for the future. Once again, I commend the choice of the theme for BECON 2001, and wish you success in your deliberations. In a fundamental sense, regulators and supervisors are under the greatest pressures of change and bear the larger responsibility for the future. For both the regulators and the regulated, eternal vigilance is the price of growth with financial stability.

9

Indian Banking System by International Standards

INTRODUCTION

An important development in this regard has been the move to set up universally acceptable standards and codes for benchmarking domestic financial systems. Moreover, multilateral assessments of country performance are increasingly focusing on observance of standards.

The IMF's Article IV consultations, its Financial Sector Stability Assessment and the Reports on Observance of Standards and Codes of the IMF and the World Bank are indicative of the fact that a country's adherence to benchmark standards and codes is being considered integral to the preservation of international monetary and financial stability. While the process has begun with the predominant involvement of governments and regulators, the search for standards and codes is progressively encompassing the private sector with consideration of issues rel ating to market discipline, corporate governance, insolvency procedures and credit rights. The impetus given to the strengthening of domestic financial systems and the international financial architecture by the Asian crisis has gathered momentum in recent years. It is important to recognise that new standards and codes are not being regarded as final goals but as instruments or enabling conditions for enhancing efficiency in financial intermediation while ensuring financial stability. There are three levels at which action is necessary, viz., legal, policy and procedures, and market practices by participants. In several areas, fundamental changes in the legal and institutional infrastructure are pre-requisites. Since these changes can impinge upon the socio-cultural as well as politico-economic ethos, appropriate adoption and some prioritisation in implementation are unavoidable.

We have made some noteworthy progress in generating a constructive debate on the applicability of international standards and codes to the Indian financial system. Participative consultation has been supported by internal self-assessments as well as external assessment.

In several areas, the issues are of a technical nature. Accordingly, the Standing Committee on International Standards and Codes, set up in December 1999, constituted ten Advisory Groups comprising eminent experts, generally non-official, to bring objectivity and experience into studying the applicability of relevant international codes and standards to each area of competence.

The Advisory Groups have submitted their reports. They have set out a roadmap for implementation of appropriate standard and codes in the light of existing levels of compliance, the cross-country experience, and the existing legal and institutional infrastructure. The Advisory Group on Banking Supervision has assessed the Indian banking system vis-à-vis the principles of the Basel Committee on Banking Supervision. It has found the level of compliance to be generally of a high order. The Advisory Group on Bankruptcy Laws has, inter alia, recommended a comprehensive bankruptcy code incorporating various aspects including cross-border insolvency and the repeal of the Sick Industrial Companies Act. The Advisory Group on Corporate Governance has made recommendations relating to rules and responsibilities of boards and has advised amendments to the Companies Act.

The Advisory Group on Data Dissemination has found that India's data dissemination compares favourably with many other countries and has proposed the compilation of forward-looking indicators.

The Advisory Group on Fiscal Transparency is of the view that current fiscal practices meet the IMF's Code of Good Practices on Fiscal Transparency. It has recommended amplifying the scope of fiscal responsibility legislation in order to include the essential elements of a budget law. The Advisory Group on Insurance regulation has recommended flexible minimum capital requirements depending on the class of business.

With regard to actuarial and solvency issues, the Group has found the Indian standards to be at par with international norms. The Advisory Group on International Accounting and Auditing Standards has set out an agenda for the future for convergence in auditing and accounting practices. It has recommended a single standard setting authority and the need for convergence of corporate and tax l aws.

The Advisory Group on Transparency in Monetary and Financial Policies has recommended inflation as the single mandated objective for the central bank and necessary autonomy to fulfill the mandate. It has also made recommendations on the operating procedures of monetary policy.

The Advisory Group on Payments and Settlement has recommended legal reforms to empower the Reserve Bank to supervise the payment and settlement system, application of the Lamfalussy standards to deferred net settlement (DNS) and introduction of Real Time Gross Settlement (RTGS). It has also recommended the setting up of the Clearing Corporation and a separate guarantee fund for foreign exchange clearing. The Advisory Group on Securities Market Regulation has compared India against the International Organisation of

Securities Commissions (IOSCO) principles and emphasised the need to strengthen inter-regulator cooperation.

Thus, in India, we have made considerable progress in the identification of international standards and codes in relevant areas, expert assessment regarding their applicability, including comparator country evaluation and building up possible course of action for the future. The next step is to sensitise all concerned - policy makers, regulators and market participants - to the issues involved and to seek the widest possible debate on issues as well as expert assessments with a view to generating a broad consensus on implementation of a universally recognised set of codes and standards.

BANKING AND FINANCE

In my inaugural address last year, I had indicated a vision for Indian banking in the new millennium - that of a vibrant, internationally active banking system, drawing upon its innate strengths and comparative advantages to make India a major banking centre of the world. I had pointed out then that, while it may take up to 10 or even 15 years to achieve this vision, the time to begin was now. Recent developments have only served to bring forward the urgency attached to embarking upon this quest. Even as we do so, it is necessary to recognise that, in view of recent global developments and the economic slowdown, the progress towards this goal would call for even greater effort and determination. In this context, the theme chosen for this year's Conference i.e., "Indian Banking: Paradigm Shift" is most timely as it provides an opportunity to deliberate on the new challenges ahead, and the action that we must take to manage them. I am happy to be a part of these deliberat ions and to deliver the inaugural address to the 23rd Conference of Bank Economists here today.

As you are aware, global economic prospects turned sharply adverse since September 2001 following the terrorist attacks on the US. The possibilities of a recovery in the global economy have become highly uncertain, belying the initial expectations of a V-shaped recovery as well as the subsequent hopes of a U-shaped recovery. As of now, the consensus of forecasts settles around 2.4 per cent for world GDP growth for 2001. World trade volume growth could slow down to around 1.3 per cent and net capital outflows from developing countries may now be larger than anticipated earlier. Although the sharp spurt in international oil prices has abated, their future behaviour remains unclear. Macroeconomic weaknesses have also been associated with an erosion of business confidence. Insurance, airlines, tourism and hotel industries have been hit hard and the exposure of financial institutions to these industries can be a potential source of vulnerability.

Despite the relatively inward-looking nature of the Indian economy, it cannot remain insulated from these international developments. The direct effects of these external developments on our banking system are expected to be limited. Indirect effects, especially through exports and subdued industrial activity could, however, impact upon the asset quality of our banking system and other segments of the financial system. The need to constantly monitor international developments and take appropriate and often, preemptive action add an entirely new dimension to the progress of our banking system towards its longer-term vision.

We have made considerable progress in implementing banking and financial sector reforms. There is also some improvement in the financial performance of the banking system in terms of various indicators of operating efficiency. Nevertheless, there are several areas regarding the efficiency of our banking system - rather than its stability - that raise concerns, especially during a period of generalised uncertainty. The level of non-performing assets (NPAs) continues be high by international standards, preempting funds for provisioning and eating into the performance and profitability of financial intermediaries. The response to the debt recovery and asset restructuring initiatives undertaken as part of financial sector reforms has also been slow.

In the period ahead, our financial system will also have to prepare for a tightening of the prudential norms as the new Basel Accord becomes effective and a fuller response to the current financial environment emerges. Our financial institutions continue to be susceptible to financial market turbulence, especially in the equity market. Upgrading technical skills, technology, research and human capital, developing effective 'front-office' strategies and fortifying internal rules of governance and responsibility assumes a renewed priority in the fast changing scenario.

The face of banking, as we have known it, is also changing rapidly. India is approaching an era of financial conglomorisation and 'bundling' in the provision of financial services. Besides infusing heightened competition, there are implications for the regulatory and supervisory regime. Banks and financial institutions have to prepare for changes in the regulatory framework towards a more focussed, comprehensive and efficient environment that eschews regulatory forbearance. Legal reforms accordingly will have to ascend the hierarchy of priorities in the reform process.

Against this background, in this talk, I propose to focus on the main challenges facing Indian banking, such as, the role of financial intermediation in different phases of the business cycle, the emerging compulsions of the new prudential norms, and benchmarking the Indian financial system against international standards and best practices. I will also say a few words about the changing context of regulation and supervision of the financial system in India, the need for introducing new technology in the banking and financial system, and the importance of strengthening skills and intellectual capital formation in the banking industry.

RECENT MACROECONOMIC DEVELOPMENTS AND THE BANKING SYSTEM

For a greater part of the twentieth century, the role of the financial system was perceived as mobilising the massive resource requirements for growth. Since the 1970s and 1980s, development economics underwent a paradigm shift. The financial system is no longer viewed as a passive mobiliser of funds. Efficiency in financial intermediation i.e., the ability of financial institutions to intermediate between savers and investors, to set economic prices for capital and to allocate resources among competing demands is now emphasised. Developments in endogenous growth theory since the late 1980s indicate that efficiency in financial intermediation is a source of technical progress to be exploited for generating increasing returns and sustaining high growth. These changes have provided the rationale for many developing countries to undertake wide-ranging reforms of their financial systems so as to prepare them for their true resource allocation function. As important financial inte rmediaries, banks have a special role to play in this new dispensation.

The sharp downturn in global macroeconomic prospects and the continuing sluggishness in domestic industrial activity have necessitated a revision in the forecast for India's real GDP growth in 2001-02 from 6.0-6.5 per cent expected at the time of the April 2001 Monetary and Credit Policy Statement to 5.0-6.0 per cent in the mid-term review of the policy. The downward revision is primarily predicated on the outlook for the industrial sector which grew by barely 2.2 per cent in April-October 2001 as against 5.9 per cent in the corresponding period of last year, mainly on account of the slowdown in manufacturing and mining and quarrying. Capital goods production declined by as much as 6.6 per cent and several sectors recorded a slow down in growth rate or an absolute decline. On the other hand, agriculture sector, supported by reasonable monsoon, recorded a rebound in growth. The kharif output is expected to cross a new peak of 105.6 million tonnes and prospects for the rabi crop are also good. On the external front, merchandise exports increased marginally by 0.5 per cent in the first eight months of 2001-02. While oil imports fell by 13.4 per cent, the non-oil imports showed an increase of 8.4 per cent. Despite a moderate widening of the trade deficit, continuing buoyancy in net invisible receipts has kept the current account deficit very low. According to available data, net capital flows are also likely to be of a higher order than in the preceding year. Foreign exchange reserves rose to US $ 48.0 billion as on December 28, 2001 recording an accretion of the order of the US $ 5.8 billion over the end-March 2001 level.

In the context of the recent deceleration in the economy the intermediation role assumes even greater relevance. Banks and financial institutions should endeavour to play a 'supply-leading' rather than 'demand-following' role in initiating the upturn by energising the financial intermediation process. By virtue of a bird's eye view of the economy and their superior credit assessment of the investment proposals and the efficiency of capital, banks should endeavour to economise on 'search' costs in identifying and nurturing growth impulses in the commodity and service producing sectors of the economy.

In the recent period, monetary policy in India has also moved into a counter-cyclical stance signalled by cuts in key interest rates and cash reserve requirements. At the same time, market operations have ensured adequate liquidity to support the revival of aggregate demand with a clear preference for softening of interest rates within the overall institutional constraints on the interest rate regime. Inflation has been steadily falling and this has had a positive impact on inflation expectations, along with the underlying resilience of the macroeconomic fundamentals of the Indian economy. The 50 basis point reduction in the Bank Rate and the 200 basis point reduction in the CRR, announced recently, are expected to significantly enhance the lendable resources of the banking system.

The current situation of comfortable liquidity provides an opportunity for banks to transform idle liquidity into investible resources for growth. The easy interest rate environment would make it possible for banks to 'price in' projects which would have earlier remained unfunded due to inherently lower returns to capital or due to lack of access to prime lending rates. This will, however, require reassessment of portfolios and internal liquidity constraints, even adjustments in risk profiles and risk management. The deceleration in the industrial growth scenario, of course, opens up the moral hazard of adverse selection and the possibilities of large-scale contamination of portfolios. In a situation of generalised slowdown, unviable projects can look potentially bankable given the scarcity of investment avenues.

Nevertheless, the possibilities for financial intermediation in the current situation are too varied and challenging to ignore. There is no systematic evidence that financial sector reforms by themselves and without supportive policies in other areas, can contribute to a revival of the economy; yet this is a time when the responsibility on the financial system to contribute to the process of economic revival is greater than before. Periods of downturn in economic activity also provide opportunities for banks to undertake consolidation and strengthening. There is a strong complementarity between financial stability and macroeconomic stability. The interests of both are served by a stable and resilient financial system.

In recent years, various measures have been taken to improve the functioning of different segments of the financial markets and thereby, to improve the operational effectiveness of monetary policy. The Liquidity Adjustment Facility (LAF), which was introduced in June 2000 has emerged as an effective and flexible instrument for managing liquidity on a day-to-day basis. In the second stage of the LAF, which commenced from May 2001, variable rate repo auctions replaced the collateralised lending facility and Level I support to primary dealers. Standing facilities were rationalised and a back-stop facility was introduced at variable market-related rates. Concurrently, LAF operating procedures were recast to improve operational flexibility and complementary measures were undertaken to improve the functioning of money and government securities market segments and to facilitate their orderly integration.

In order to enable the call money market to evolve into a pure inter-bank market, lending by non-banks was reduced to 85 per cent of their average daily call lending in 2000-01 from May 2001. The minimum maturity for wholesale term deposits of Rs.15 lakh and above has been reduced to 7 days from the earlier minimum maturity of 15 days. The maintenance of daily minimum cash reserve requirements has been lowered to 50 per cent from 65 per cent for the first seven days of the reporting fortnight. Interest paid on eligible balances under CRR has been raised to the level of the Bank Rate from November 3, 2001. The market has responded positively with an appreciable rise in turnover and a decline in volatility.

Several measures have also been taken to improve the functioning of the government securities market. 14-day and 182-day Treasury Bills were withdrawn and the notified amounts of 91-day Treasury Bills has been simultaneously increased. A Negotiated Dealing System (NDS) is being introduced to facilitate electronic bidding and to disseminate information on trades on a real-time basis. For this purpose, the Reserve Bank has begun the automation of its public debt offices. An important step is the setting up of the Clearing Corporation of India Ltd. (CCIL) to act as counterparty in all trades involving government securities, Treasury Bills, repos and foreign exchange. The entire system will operate in a networked environment and INdian FInancial NETwork (INFINET) will provide the backbone for communication.

PRUDENTIAL NORMS

A strong and resilient financial system and the orderly evolution of financial markets are key prerequisites for financial stability and economic progress. In keeping with the vision of an internationally competitive and sound banking system, deepening and broadening of prudential norms to the best internationally recognised standards have been the core of our approach to financial sector reforms. This has been supported concurrently by heightened market discipline, pro-active and comprehensive supervision of the financial system and the orderly development of financial market segments.

The calibration of the convergence with international standards is conditioned by the specific realities of our situation; however, the New Capital Accord of the Basel Committee on Banking Supervision which was released in January 2001 adds urgency to the process of convergence. It is against the backdrop of these exigencies that prudential norms are being constantly monitored and refined.

In the rec ent period, banks are being encouraged to build risk-weighted components of their subsidiaries into their own balance sheets and to assign additional capital. Risk weights are being constantly refined to take into recognition additional sources of risk. The concept of 'past due' in the identification of NPAs has been dispensed with. Banks and financial institutions are being urged to prepare to move to the international practice of the '90 day norm' in the classification of assets as non-performing by 2003-04.

The new Basel Accord, as contained in the second Consultative Paper on Capital Adequacy of the Basel Committee on Banking Supervision released in January 2001 is in response to the perceived rigidities in the 1988 Accord's capital requirements, the scope for capital arbitrage and the increased sophistication in the measurement and management of risk. The new Accord rests on three mutually reinforcing pillars i.e., minimum capital requirements, processes of supervisory review and market discipline. Under the first pillar, the current definition of capital and the minimum requirement of 8 per cent of capital to risk weighted assets is retained. Capital requirements would be extended on a consolidated basis to holding companies of banking groups.

The primary emphasis of the new Accord is on improving the measurement of risk. The process of measurement of market risk is maintained. Three alternatives for calculating credit risk capital requirements are proposed to be made available to banks, depending on the complexity of their business and the quality of their risk management operations.

The 'standardised approach' which can be employed by less complex banks remains conceptually the same as in the 1988 norms; however, it expands the scale of risk weights and uses external credit ratings to categorise credits. Banks with more advanced risk management capabilities can employ an internal ratings based (IRB) approach - 'foundation' and 'advanced' variants are proposed on a progression scale - in which banks may categorise exposures into multiple credit ratings of their approved internal rating systems. The internally estimated probability of default, the maturity of exposure and the credit type i.e., corporate or retail, will det ermine risk weights. There is a new explicit capital charge proposed on operational risk.

The processes of supervisory review contained in the second pillar emphasise the need for banks to develop sound internal procedures to assess the adequacy of capital based on a thorough evaluation of its risk profile and control environment, and to set commensurate targets for capital. The internal processes would be subject to supervisory evaluation, review and intervention, when appropriate.

The third pillar aims at bolstering market discipline through enhanced disclosure by banks. Disclosure requirements are set out in several areas under the new Accord, including the way in which banks calculate their capital adequacy and their risk assessment methods.

The Basel Committee on Banking Supervision has received more than 250 comments on the January 2001 proposals. The Committee is expected to release a fully specified proposal, based on these comments, in early 2002 and to finalise the Accord during 2002. An implementation date of 2005 is envisaged.

The Reserve Bank forwarded its comments to the Basel committee in May 2001. It has supported flexibility, discretion to national supervisors and a phased approach in implementing the Accord.

The Accord could initially apply to internationally active - banks with over 15 per cent of their business in cross-border transactions, as proposed by the Reserve Bank - and significant banks whose domestic market share exceeds 1 per cent - with a simplified standardised approach to be evolved for other banks. Material limits on cross-holdings of capital and eschewing of direct responsibility on external credit rating agencies in the assessment of bank assets have also been proposed by the Reserve Bank. It has also expressed its preference for external credit rating agencies that publicly disclose risk scores, rating processes and methodologies.

The new accord, when implemented, is likely to have significant implications for the banking system as a whole. Besides requiring increased capital, it attaches urgency to the development of efficient and comprehensive internal systems for assessment and management of risks, setting up and adhering to adequate internal exposure limits and improving internal control generally.

The guidelines for risk management and asset liability management provided by the Reserve Bank serve as a useful foundation for building more sophisticated control systems.

The feedback received from few banks indicates the need for substantial upgradation of existing management information systems, risk management practices and technical skills.

Capital allocation is also expected to be more risk sensitive and, therefore, banks and financial institutions will have to plan in advance so that there are no disruptions in the capital structure. Further sophistication in risk management and control mechanisms will have to evolve as experience with preferential risk-weighting and sensitivity to external ratings is accumulated.

A key requirement when the new Accord, after further modification, becomes operational is that of high quality human resources to cope with and adapt to the new environment. Enhancing technical skills and abilities to handle new technologies and new risks, exploiting information flows to price them in, and developing foresight in anticipating changing risk-return relationships will become essential.

MARKET DISCIPLINE

Processes of transparency and market disclosure of critical information describing the risk profile, capital structure and capital adequacy are assuming increasing importance in the emerging environment.

Besides making banks more accountable and responsive to better-informed investors, these processes enable banks to strike the right balance between risks and rewards and to improve the access to markets. Improvements in market discipline also call for greater coordination between banks and regulators.

India has been a participant in the international initiatives to ensure improved processes of market discipline that are being worked out in several fora, such as, the multilateral organisations, the BIS, the Financial Stability Forum, and the Core Principles Liaison Group.

Concurrent efforts are underway to refine and upgrade financial information monitoring and flow, data dissemination and data warehousing.

Banks are currently required to disclose in their balance sheets information on maturity profiles of assets and liabilities, lending to sensitive sectors, movements in NPAs, besides providing information on capital, provisions, shareholdings of the government, value of investments in India and abroad, and other operating and profitability indicators.

Financial institutions are also required to meet these disclosure norms. Banks also have to disclose their total investments made in equity shares, units of mutual funds, bonds and debentures, and aggregate advances against shares in their notes to balance sheets.

From this year onwards, notes to banks' balance sheets will disclose the movement of provisions against NPAs as well as those held towards depreciation on investments. Guidelines relating to non-SLR investments through the private placement route mandate the disclosure of information on issuer composition and non-performing investments in a similar manner. Efforts have been made to identify and monitor early warning indicators of financial crises.

The overall approach is to combine the use of micro-prudential indicators with macro-economic indicators in order to develop a set of aggregate macro-prudential indicators. This brings about a mix between bottom-up and top-down assessment.

As the methodology gets refined and the indicators are stress-tested for predictive power, financial stability surveillance will be significantly improved. This process will involve greater transparency and objectivity in the disclosure practices of banks.

Efforts have also been made to set up a Credit Information Bureau to collect and share information on borrowers and improve the credit appraisal of banks and financial institutions within the ambit of the existing legislation.

The Bureau has been incorporated by the State Bank of India in collaboration with Housing Development Finance Corporation (HDFC) and foreign technology partners.

Collection and sharing of some items of information have already been initiated. Efforts are also going into the collection and sharing of information on private placement of debt under the Bureau so that there is greater transparency in such trades.

The possibility of collecting and disseminating information on suit-filed accounts by the Bureau (in place of the Reserve

Bank) is being explored by a Working Group constituted for this purpose with representation from across the financial system. The Group will also examine the prospects of on-line supply of information and the processing of queries. A draft leg islation covering various aspects of information sharing, including issues relating to rights, responsibilities, and privacy has been prepared, which would considerably strengthen the functioning of the Bureau when it is enacted.

10

Credit Credition of Baniking

INTRODUCTION

Modern central banking allows multiple banks to practice fractional reserve banking with inter-bank business transactions without risking bankruptcy. The process of fractional-reserve banking has a cumulative effect of money creation by banks, essentially expanding the money supply of the economy.

There are two types of money in a fractional-reserve banking system operating with a central bank.

1. central bank money (money created or adopted by the central bank regardless of its form (precious metals, commodity certificates, banknotes, coins, electronic money loaned to commercial banks, or anything else the central bank chooses as its form of money)
2. commercial bank money (demand deposits in the commercial banking system) - sometimes referred to as chequebook money.

When a deposit of central bank money is made at a commercial bank, the central bank money is removed for circulation, and an equal amount of new commercial bank money is created. When a loan is made using the central bank money from the commercial bank (which keeps only a fraction of the central bank money as reserves), the money supply expands by the size of the loan.

The table below displays how loans are funded and how the money supply is affected. It also shows how central bank money is used to create commercial bank money from an initial deposit of $100 of central bank money. In the example, the initial deposit is lent out 10 times with a fractional-reserve rate of 20% to ultimately create $400 of commercial bank money. Each bank involved in this process creates new commercial bank money on only a portion of the original deposit of central bank money, ensuring that it always has enough reserves on hand to meet the inter-bank business demands, and also ensuring that multiple banks participate in the inflation process so that all banks are inflating at the same rate.

The process begins when an initial $100 deposit of central bank money is made into Bank A. Bank A then takes 20 percent of it, or $20, and sets it aside as reserves and then loans out the remaining 80 percent, or $80. At this point there is actually a total of $180 in the system, not $100; because the bank has loaned out $80 of the central bank money, kept $20 of central bank money in reserve, and substituted a newly created $80 IOU claim for the depositor that acts equivalent to and can be implicitly redeemed for central bank money (the depositor can transfer it to another account, write a check on it, etc.). These checkbook IOUs are termed commercial bank money and are simply recorded in a bank's register as an asset (specifically, an IOU from the loan recipient) next to the reserves. From a depositor's perspective, commercial money is central bank money--it's impossible to tell the two forms of money apart until a bank run happens (at which time everyone wants central bank money). At this point Bank A still holds $100 of central bank money reserves on its books, but $80 of those reserves are soon going to be needed to satisfy the loan recipient. The loan recipient soon spends the $80. The receiver of that $80 then deposits it into Bank B. Bank B demands $80 of central bank money be delivered from Bank A to Bank B in satisfaction of the loan recipient's check. Bank A now only has $20 of central bank money on its books.

Bank B is now in the same situation as Bank A started with, except it has a deposit of $80 of central bank money instead of $100. Similar to Bank A, Bank B sets aside 20 percent of that $80, or $16, as reserves and lends out the remaining $64, creating $64 of IOUs to its depositors. As the process continues, more commercial bank money is created. To simplify the table, a different bank is used for each deposit. In the real world, the money a bank lends may end up in the same bank so it then has more money to lend out.

Although no new money was physically created in addition to the initial $100 deposit, new commercial bank money is created through loans. The 2 boxes marked in red show the location of the original $100 deposit throughout the entire process. The total reserves plus the last deposit (or last loan, whichever is last) will always equal the original amount, which in this case is $100. As this process continues, more commercial bank money is created.

The amounts in each step decrease towards a limit. If a graph is made showing the accumulation of deposits, one can see that the graph is curved and approaches a limit. This limit is the maximum amount of money that can be created with a given reserve rate. When the reserve rate is 20%, as in the example above, the maximum amount of total deposits that can be created is $500 and the maximum amount of commercial bank money that can be created is $400.

For an individual bank, the deposit is considered a liability whereas the loan it gives out and the reserves are considered assets. The deposit will always be equal to the loan plus the reserve, since the loan and reserve are created from the deposit. This is the basis for a bank's balance sheet.

The creation and destruction of commercial bank money occurs through this process. Whether it is created or destroyed depends on what direction the process moves. When loans are given out, the process moves from the top down and money is created. When loans are paid back, the process moves from the bottom to the top and commercial bank money is canceled out, effectively erasing it from existence.

This table gives an outline of the makeup of money supplies worldwide. Most of the money in any given money supply consists of commercial bank money. The value of commercial bank money comes from the fact that it can be exchanged at a bank for central bank money.

This is a general outline of how it works. The actual increase in the money supply through this process may be lower, as (at each step) banks may choose to hold reserves in excess of the statutory minimum, borrowers may let some funds sit idle, and some borrowers may choose to hold cash, and there may be delays or frictions in the process. It may also be higher if the reserve requirement is lower or if there are no reserve requirements. Government regulations may also be used to limit the money creation process by preventing banks from giving out loans even though the reserve requirements have been fulfilled.

AN ANALYSIS OF INDIAN COMMERCIAL BANKING INDUSTRY

The index of industrial production (IIP) rose by 9.8 per cent during April-August 2007 as against 11.0 per cent in the corresponding period last year. Manufacturing output increased by 10.3 per cent (12.2 per cent a year ago) while mining activity and electricity generation rose by 5.4 per cent (3.0 per cent) and 8.3 per cent (5.7 per cent), respectively. Manufacturing activity was led by food products, wood products, chemicals, basic metals and alloys and non-transport machinery and equipments which together constituted 53.9 per cent of the manufacturing sector and contributed 71.5 per cent of its growth during April-August 2007. On the other hand, deceleration in the production of textiles and transport equipment, and decline in the production of metal products and parts which have a combined share of 22.3 per cent in the manufacturing sector, had a moderating effect on manufacturing activity as well as on overall industrial growth during this period.

The use-based classification indicates sustained investment demand as reflected in an increase of 21.3 per cent (19.5 per cent) in capital goods production. Production of basic goods and intermediate goods increased by 10.0 per cent (8.3 per cent) and 9.3 per cent (10.4 per cent), respectively. Consumer goods growth decelerated to 6.2 per cent (11.4 per cent), mainly due to a decline of 2.3 per cent in the consumer durables. The six infrastructure industries, which together comprise nearly 27 per cent of the IIP, posted a growth of 6.6 per cent during April-August 2007 as against 8.3 per cent a year ago. Except for electricity generation, all other sectors of core infrastructure recorded decelerated growth. Information on corporate activity indicates that sales of selected companies had risen by 19.2 per cent during April-June 2007, lower than 25.6 per cent in the corresponding quarter a year ago. The rise in other income, lower interest burden, improvements in operational efficiency, higher capacity utilisation and economies of scale appear to have contributed substantially to overall financial performance and high profit margins especially for larger companies, despite an increase of 18.1 per cent in depreciation provision. Net profits rose by 33.9 per cent in the first quarter of 2007-08 as against 34.7 per cent during the corresponding period last year. Buoyant equity markets enabled higher mobilisation of resources by the private corporate sector through public issues and private placements than in the corresponding period of 2006-07. Early results for the second quarter of 2007-08 (July-September) for a truncated sample of companies indicate continuing moderation in sales and profitability growth relative to the corresponding quarter a year ago as well as the preceding quarter, especially for manufacturing companies.

On the other hand, some decline in the interest burden on a year-on-year basis, reflecting the relatively higher recourse of corporates to external commercial borrowings (ECBs) and consequently lower interest payments relative to domestic borrowings as well as gains thereon in rupee terms due to exchange rate appreciation boosted other income and helped to shore up net profit margins. The Reserve Bank's Industrial Outlook Survey conducted mainly during August 2007, which covers private manufacturing companies, indicates stable business conditions. Half of the respondent companies reported increase in production and a better overall business situation; over 40 per cent indicated no change in these characteristics. A majority of respondents felt that capacity utilisation would remain unchanged. The overall assessment of working capital requirement, availability of finance and overall financial situation was positive for July-September 2007. The assessment of moderation in export and import growth that started in the beginning of the year continued to prevail. On a net basis, respondents reported a higher increase in input cost than in selling prices. The business expectation index for July-September 2007 improved by 3.1 percentage points from its level in the previous quarter; however, it was lower by 1.8 percentage points from its level a year ago. For October-December 2007, the business expectation index rose by 3.3 percentage points from its level in the previous quarter though lower by 0.9 percentage points on a year-on-year basis. Over a fifth of respondents expect increase in employment level in their companies during July-December 2007. While 60 per cent did not expect any change in profit margins, a fourth of the respondents expected increase in profitability.

Other business confidence surveys which also cover services sector companies present a somewhat mixed picture. According to one survey, business confidence shows a fall of 8.9 percentage points in July-December 2007 relative to its level in the previous round, reflecting some increase in the cost of finance and rising prices of raw materials. A lower level of confidence in overall economic conditions and industry/firm level performance is also reflected in some other surveys. On the other hand, some surveys report optimism on value of production, new orders and utilisation of capacity for the second half of 2007-08. In this view, seasonally adjusted purchasing managers' indices, which cover only manufacturing companies, point to a robust improvement in operating conditions with marked increase in output and new orders, underpinned by favourable domestic market conditions. Price increases for both inputs and outputs were stated to be high by respondents but were not expected to impede the step-up in purchasing activity and hiring of additional staff due to higher production requirements.

Lead indicators suggest that the pace of expansion in the services sector activity has been sustained during April-August 2007. The communication sector has recorded robust growth with 34 million telephone connections (fixed plus cellular) in April-August 2007 which is 55.4 per cent higher than 22 million connections provided in the corresponding period last year. Cargo handled at major ports increased by 14.2 per cent, whereas handling of import cargo and export cargo in the civil aviation sector increased by 23.5 per cent and 5.4 per cent, respectively. Railway revenue earnings from freight traffic increased by 7.0 per cent which was lower than the growth of 9.9 per cent in the corresponding period last year, mainly due to lower traffic for carriage of foodgrains and raw materials for steel plants. Passengers handled at domestic and international terminals increased by 27.8 per cent and 12.4 per cent, respectively, as against 40.1 per cent and 12.9 per cent a year ago.

According to the CSO's end-August 2007 release, there are indications of underlying shifts in the constituents of aggregate demand. As a proportion to GDP, real private final consumption expenditure declined to 58.8 per cent during the first quarter of 2007-08 from 60.8 per cent a year ago. On the other hand, real gross fixed capital formation (GFCF) increased to 29.6 per cent of GDP from 27.9 per cent, indicative of the investment led acceleration of growth in the Indian economy. As regards external demand, net exports are placed at (-)1.0 per cent of GDP in April-June 2007 vis-à-vis 0.8 per cent a year ago.

On a year-on-year basis, total credit extended by scheduled commercial banks (SCBs) increased by Rs.3,81,333 crore (23.3 per cent) up to October 12, 2007 as compared with an increase of Rs.3,66,463 crore (28.8 per cent) a year ago. On a financial year basis, credit extended by SCBs increased by Rs.90,262 crore (4.7 per cent) up to October 12, 2007 as compared with the increase of Rs.1,30,764 crore (8.7 per cent) in the corresponding period last year. Food credit declined by Rs.9,501 crore as against a decline of Rs.7,246 crore in the previous year. Non-food credit registered an increase of Rs.99,763 crore (5.3 per cent) as compared with an increase of Rs.1,38,010 crore (9.4 per cent) in the corresponding period of the previous year.

Provisional information available from select SCBs up to August 2007 indicates that credit to industries expanded by 24.6 per cent up to August on a year-on-year basis, slowing from 25.7 per cent in March 2007. Credit to agriculture expanded by 24.4 per cent (32.4 per cent in March 2007). On the other hand, bank credit to services and personal loans at 24.5 per cent (31.0 per cent) and 19.8 per cent (26.5 per cent), respectively, recorded a sizeable slowdown. Within the industrial sector, credit off-take by infrastructure, chemicals and vehicles and auto parts picked up to 32.1 per cent (26.8 per cent), 16.1 per cent (14.2 per cent) and 28.5 per cent (11.0 per cent), respectively. On the other hand, credit disbursed decelerated in the case of textiles to 28.0 per cent (34.2 per cent), metals to 19.6 per cent (26.7 per cent), engineering to 24.0 per cent (24.5 per cent) and petroleum to 35.7 per cent (41.0 per cent).

In the services sector, all constituents barring computer software, tourism and hotels and non-banking financial companies recorded deceleration in credit off-take. In particular, growth in credit to real estate decelerated to 52.9 per cent from 69.8 per cent in March 2007, but still remained high. Under personal loans, sizeable deceleration in credit occurred under housing (to 16.6 per cent in August 2007 from 24.6 per cent in March 2007), consumer durables (to 4.1 per cent from 28.9 per cent) and other personal loans (to 22.5 per cent from 30.3

per cent).

Credit to industry recorded the highest share of 41.1 per cent in total incremental non-food bank credit by August 2007, followed by services (23.8 per cent), personal loans (22.4 per cent) and agriculture (12.7 per cent). The shares of infrastructure, engineering and chemical industries in incremental credit to industry increased from 21.4 per cent, 6.0 per cent and 4.9 per cent, respectively, in March 2007 to 26.7 per cent, 6.2 per cent and 5.5 per cent in August 2007. The share of metals, textiles, petroleum and food processing declined from 12.4 per cent, 14.1 per cent, 7.3 per cent and 6.1 per cent, respectively, to 10.0 per cent, 12.4 per cent, 6.2 per cent and 6.0 per cent. The share of the priority sector in incremental non-food gross bank credit declined marginally to 31.0 per cent from 31.2 per cent. Priority sector advances rose by 20.2 per cent up to August 2007, lower than 24.0 per cent in March 2007. While the share of agriculture declined to 12.7 per cent in August 2007 from 14.4 per cent in March 2007, the share of small scale industries (SSIs) increased to 8.3 per cent from 6.6 per cent. There has been a greater deceleration in credit disbursements in respect of the services and retail sectors as compared with industry.

On a year-on-year basis, commercial banks' investments in shares, bonds/debentures and commercial paper (CP) declined by Rs.5,514 crore (6.7 per cent) up to October 12, 2007 as compared with a decline of Rs.895 crore (1.1 per cent) a year ago. On a financial year basis, such investments by banks fell by Rs.6,930 crore (8.5 per cent) during 2007-08 so far (up to October 12), as against an increase of Rs.2,514 crore (3.2 per cent) in the corresponding period of 2006-07. Banks' investments in instruments issued by all-India financial institutions and mutual funds, however, increased by Rs.49,847 crore as against an increase of Rs.11,526 crore in the corresponding period of the previous year. The year-on-year growth in total resource flow from SCBs to the commercial sector was 22.1 per cent, over and above the growth of 28.0 per cent a year ago. In addition, during the first quarter of the current financial year, corporates raised additional resources in the form of external commercial borrowings (ECBs) amounting to Rs.29,498 crore as against Rs.18,882 crore in the first quarter last year.

On an annual basis, the growth in aggregate deposits at 24.9 per cent (Rs.5,69,061 crore) was higher than that of 20.4 per cent (Rs.3,88,528 crore) a year ago. On a financial year basis, aggregate deposits of SCBs increased by 9.6 per cent (Rs.2,49,724 crore) up to October 12, 2007 as compared with an increase of 8.5 per cent (Rs.1,79,923 crore) in the corresponding period of the previous year. Reflecting high profitability and internal generation of resources by the corporate sector, its share in total deposits with the banking system has been increasing, mainly in the form of short-term deposits. On the other hand, the share of savings deposits in total deposits has been declining. The incremental annual non-food credit-deposit ratio declined to 66.4 per cent on October 12, 2007 from 95.3 per cent a year ago.

Movements in the key monetary and banking aggregates in the second quarter of 2007-08 were reflected in generally easy conditions of liquidity, except for some short-lived episodes of tightness. The banking system experienced conditions of surplus liquidity on account of substantial deposit mobilisation relative to credit demand as well as capital augmentation through several large IPOs. Consequently, banks made sizeable investments in Government securities/Treasury bills issued under the MSS. With effect from August 6, 2007 the daily ceiling of Rs.3,000 crore on reverse repo under the LAF stipulated since March 5, 2007 was removed. During August 6-31, 2007 average daily net absorption under the LAF was Rs.25,333 crore, despite an additional amount of Rs.13,500 crore absorbed under the MSS.

On August 9, 2007 the Reserve Bank transferred its annual profit to the Central Government which included a one-time payment of Rs.34,309 crore on account of profit on sale of the Reserve Bank's stake in the State Bank of India (SBI) which augmented the Central Government's cash balances with the Reserve Bank. Large absorption of liquidity under the LAF and the MSS continued till the third week of September when quarterly advance tax outflows and build-up of the Centre's cash balances led to a sharp drop in the daily volumes of funds offered at the LAF auctions, and the Reserve Bank had to inject liquidity under the LAF on September 21 and 28. In view of large capital inflows, an additional amount of Rs.68,685 crore was sterilised during September and October under the MSS with the outstanding sterilisation under the MSS increasing to Rs.1,77,155 crore by October 26, 2007.

The overhang of liquidity as reflected in the sum of LAF, MSS and the Central Governments' cash balances increased from Rs.85,770 crore at end-March 2007 to Rs.1,24,632 crore on August 6, 2007 and further to Rs.2,22,582 crore by October 24, 2007. The Government of India, in consultation with the Reserve Bank, revised the ceiling under MSS for the year 2007-08 from Rs.1,10,000 crore to Rs.1,50,000 crore on August 8, 2007 and further to Rs.2,00,000 crore on October 4, 2007.

In view of the lower credit growth, banks undertook incremental investment in statutory liquidity ratio (SLR) securities. SCBs' investment in SLR securities at Rs.1,52,488 crore during the current financial year up to October 12, 2007 was higher than that of Rs.49,717 crore in the corresponding period of the previous year. The ratio of such investments to aggregate deposits on an incremental basis was 30.9 per cent as against 6.1 per cent in the corresponding period last year. It needs to be mentioned that a part of this increase was due to bank recapitalisation bonds (amounting to Rs.5,270 crore) being considered as approved securities for SLR, and part due to subscription to SLR bonds issued under the market stabilisation scheme (MSS). Even after adjusting for banks' repo/reverse repo with the Reserve Bank under the Liquidity Adjustment Facility (LAF), SLR investments at Rs.86,758 crore during 2007-08 so far were much higher than the increase of Rs.38,727 crore in the corresponding period last year.

Consequently, on an outstanding basis, commercial banks' holdings of Government and other approved securities increased to 30.0 per cent of their net demand and time liabilities (NDTL) as on October 12, 2007 from 28.0 per cent at end-March 2007. While these investments exceeded the required SLR by Rs.1,56,851 crore (Rs.84,223 crore at end-March 2007), the excess SLR investment adjusted for LAF holdings amounted to Rs.1,20,306 crore or 3.8 per cent of NDTL.

Year-on-year money supply (M3) at 21.8 per cent as on October 12, 2007 was higher than 18.9 per cent a year ago and above the range of 17.0-17.5 per cent indicated in the Annual Policy Statement of April 2007. On a financial year basis, M3 increased by 8.2 per cent (Rs.2,72,010 crore) up to October 12, 2007 as compared with the increase of 7.7 per cent (Rs.2,11,279 crore) in the corresponding period of the previous year.

Reserve money increased by 24.4 per cent on a year-on-year as on October 19, 2007 as compared with 20.2 per cent a year ago. On a financial year basis, reserve money increased by 8.0 per cent (Rs.57,060 crore) up to October 19, 2007 as compared with the increase of 7.5 per cent (Rs.42,932 crore) in the corresponding period of the previous year. The large increase in reserve money in the current financial year so far reflects in part the initial impact of recent increases in the cash reserve ratio (CRR). Among the components of reserve money, therefore, bankers' deposits with the Reserve Bank increased by 18.7 per cent (Rs.36,984 crore) during the current year so far as compared with an increase of 5.2 per cent (Rs.7,047 crore) in the corresponding period last year. Currency in circulation, however, registered a lower growth of 4.5 per cent (Rs.22,589 crore) as compared with 8.7 per cent (Rs.37,319 crore).

Among the sources of reserve money, Reserve Bank's net credit to the Central Government declined by Rs.1,43,116 crore as compared with an increase of Rs.15,029 crore in the corresponding period last year. Adjusted for transactions under the LAF, Reserve Bank's credit to the Central Government showed a decline of Rs.81,981 crore mainly on account of increased MSS issuance in 2007-08 so far. The Reserve Bank's net foreign exchange assets (NFEA) increased by Rs.1,71,080 crore as against an increase of Rs.77,310 crore during the corresponding period of the previous year. Adjusted for revaluation, NFEA increased by Rs.2,17,201 crore as compared with an increase of Rs.42,544 crore during the corresponding period of the previous year. The ratio of NFEA to currency increased from 171.8 per cent on March 31, 2007 to 196.9 per cent by October 19, 2007.

Benefiting from favourable south-west monsoon conditions, the area sown under kharif rice, pulses and oilseeds increased to 37.3 million hectares, 12.5 million hectares and 17.8 million hectares, respectively, up to October 19, 2007 as against 37.1 million hectares, 11.4 million hectares and 16.8 million hectares in the 2006 season. Acreage under cash crops such as cotton, jute and sugarcane was also higher than a year ago. First advance estimates released by the Ministry of Agriculture place kharif foodgrains production at 112.2 million tonnes, below the target of 114.2 million tonnes, but higher than 110.5 million tonnes recorded last year. As per these initial estimates, production of nine major oilseeds during the kharif season is placed at 16.1 million tonnes which is lower than the target of 18.5 million tonnes, but significantly higher than the output of 13.9 million tonnes in 2006-07. Production of cotton, jute and sugarcane is also expected to register an increase in 2007-08. The pace of the broadening expansion of economic activity appears to have been sustained in the second quarter of 2007-08. Lead indicators point to congenial conditions for a pick-up in agricultural activity on the back of the higher than expected growth recorded in the preceding quarter. Rainfall during the 2007 south-west monsoon season was five per cent above the long-period average (LPA) for the country as a whole according to the India Meteorological Department (IMD). Of the 36 meteorological subdivisions across the country, rainfall was excess/normal in as many as 30 sub-divisions as against 26 in the 2006 season. On the other hand, six sub-divisions which have received deficient rainfall in the 2007 season include Punjab, Haryana, Himachal Pradesh, western Uttar Pradesh and eastern Madhya Pradesh which are major foodgrains producing regions. As on October 18, 2007 live storage in 81 major reservoirs was 81 per cent of designated capacity which is 19.3 per cent higher than the last 10 years' average but 3.1 per cent lower than the level a year ago. The water storage level supports the prospects for rabi production.

IMPLICATIONS FOR BUSINESS CYCLE THEORY

For the element of Time, which is the center of the chief difficulty of almost every economic problem, is itself absolutely continuous: Nature knows no partition of time into long periods and short; but the two shade into one another by imperceptible gradations, and what is the short period for one problem is a long period for another.

While the element of time may be the chief difficulty of almost every economic problem, the difficulties are most apparent and most persistently resist generally accepted solutions in the area of monetary theory and macroeconomics. Money, which simultaneously functions as a medium of exchange and a store of value, may be viewed as the quintessential present good or as a future good, the most liquid store of value. This dual nature of money has been the center of macroeconomic controversy since the time of the classical economists. The Austrian business cycle theory is a blend of monetary and capital theory and highlights coordination problems connected to "time and money." In the framework developed by Ludwig von Mises, banks create money by creating credit. This created credit finances investment in excess of savings, distorts the structure of production, and sets the stage for the boom–bust cycle. But what is created credit and when and how do banks create credit? Different answers to this question yield different implications for business cycle theory, research, and monetary policy, as well as different monetary reform proposals. Section two examines the classical roots of the time, money,

Our main focus will be on discovering the conditions under which banks create rather than intermediate credit. Section five provides conclusions and directions for future research. But does Say's Law hold true for a monetary economy where savings and investment decisions take place under conditions in which the element of time is of critical importance? The original answers to the critics of Say's Law separated the issues of capital and money. The rate of interest could be relied upon to balance saving and investment.

While economic activity is measured in monetary units, classical economists tended to think in real terms. Saving releases resources from the provision of present goods. These resources are then available for the provision of future goods. Investment is the use of these available resources for capital formation and hence provision of future consumable goods. Summarizes, the supply of and demand for investable resources. Saving first shows up on the market explicitly as non-spending on consumable goods, but is in reality an implicit demand for future goods. Saved funds flow into capital markets where fluctuations in the rate of interest ensure that the funds saved are invested in the creation of new capital goods. A surplus of saving over investment, which could be the source of a general glut, would be merely a disequilibrium phenomenon in the capital markets. Money not spent on consumable goods could, however, be hoarded.

Households and firms could attempt to build up cash reserves by reducing planned expenditures on goods and services. These increased cash balances would not flow into the financial markets. But money is a medium of exchange and implicitly a present good. As people build up their cash balances, they are expressing a preference for real money balances over other present goods and services. Money balances become relatively more valuable and goods relatively less valuable. Money prices of goods and services fall, reflecting the new valuations of economic agents. When equilibrium is restored, goods and services sell at lower money prices. No actual saving (resources released from present provision) has taken place, nor was any real saving intended. The distribution of present goods between money and consumable goods has changed, but the margin between the demand for present goods and the demand for future goods has not changed. Mises expanded on and made explicit the classical reasoning. While he argued that money was neither a consumption good nor a production good, he definitely classified 'money' as a present good in his discussions on money and credit.

The quantity theory of money could be used to illustrate how fluctuations in money prices would balance money supply and money demand so that in a full general equilibrium no overproduction or glut would exist. Gluts or overproduction caused by either hoarding or a decline in the money supply would be a temporary maladjustment, a monetary disequilibrium phenomenon.

DOMESTIC DEVELOPMENTS

Inflation, measured by variations in the wholesale price index (WPI) on a year-on-year basis, eased from its peak of 6.4 per cent on April 07, 2007 to 3.1 per cent by October 13, 2007. On an average basis, however, annual WPI inflation at 5.2 per cent was higher than 4.6 per cent a year ago.

At a disaggregated level, prices of primary articles (weight: 22.0 per cent in the WPI basket) and manufactured products (weight: 63.8 per cent) increased by 5.2 per cent and 4.1 per cent, respectively, by October 13, 2007 as compared with an increase of 8.1 per cent and 4.6 per cent a year ago. An analysis of constituent price movements indicates that the rise in prices of edible oils, oilseeds and oilcakes, which together have a weight of 6.9 per cent in the WPI, contributed nearly 40 per cent of the headline inflation, while 16 per cent of headline inflation came from increases in prices of primary food items especially rice, milk and vegetables.

Excluding food, headline WPI inflation was 3.0 per cent as against 5.0 per cent a year ago. Other items that contributed to headline inflation included cement, drugs and medicines, iron and steel and electrical machinery.

Annual inflation of the 'fuel, power, light and lubricants' group (weight: 14.2 per cent) declined to 1.6 per cent as on October 13, 2007 as against 5.0 per cent a year ago. Excluding the fuel group, inflation was at 4.4 per cent (5.6 per cent a year ago).

The average price of the Indian basket of international crude was at around US $ 72.1 per barrel during July-September 2007 higher than US $ 66.4 in April-June 2007 and US $ 56.6 in January-March 2007. Since the last revision of domestic retail prices of petrol and diesel in February 2007, the price of the Indian basket had increased by about 32 per cent in US dollar terms and about 21 per cent in rupee terms up to September 2007.

Subsequently, there has been a further increase in crude oil prices in the international markets and the average price of the Indian crude basket has gone up to US $ 80 per barrel as on October 23, 2007. While the price of the Indian crude basket in rupee terms went up by an average of 22.4 per cent per annum between 2002-03 and 2006-07, the increase in prices of petrol and diesel and the freely priced products (such as aviation turbine fuel, furnace oil and naphtha) were 12.8 per cent and 16.5 per cent per annum, respectively.

This suggests an average pass-through of around 57 per cent in the case of petrol and diesel and around 73 per cent in the case of the freely priced products. The subsidy schemes for kerosene and domestic LPG, which were available through public distribution system (PDS) until March 2007, have been extended till March 2010. Domestic retail prices of petrol and diesel have remained unchanged after two downward revisions in 2006-07, thereby increasing the magnitude of incomplete pass-through.

The issue of oil bonds and burden sharing by upstream oil public sector units (PSUs) in the form of discounts on crude oil and products is expected to mitigate a part of the under-recoveries. Overall, inflation risks on account of oil prices remain incipient and it is possible that some increase in domestic prices of petroleum products would translate into some elevation in WPI inflation.

Inflation, based on the consumer price index (CPI) for industrial workers, showed a sharp increase to 7.3 per cent on a year-on-year basis in August 2007 from 6.3 per cent a year ago.

Year-on-year inflation based on the CPI for urban non-manual employees, agricultural labourers and rural labourers in September 2007 increased to 5.7 per cent, 7.9 per cent and 7.6 per cent, respectively, from 6.6 per cent, 7.3 per cent and 7.0 per cent a year ago.

A major portion of the differences between inflation rates based on the WPI and CPIs is explained by prices of food items which have a higher weight in the CPIs than in the WPI.

Year-on-year CPI inflation for industrial workers was 9.6 per cent for food items and 5.2 per cent for non-food items in August 2007 whereas for urban non-manual employees and agricultural labourers, it was 7.7 per cent and 8.8 per cent for food items, respectively, and 4.0 per cent and 6.0 per cent for non-food items, in September 2007.

In drawing meaningful inferences from the data on fiscal developments during the year, it is necessary to take account of the one-time transaction relating to transfer of the Reserve Bank's shareholding in the State Bank of India (SBI). On June 29, 2007 the Central Government paid Rs.35,531 crore to the Reserve Bank as consideration amount for the transfer.

On August 9, 2007 the Reserve Bank transferred an amount of Rs.45,720 crore as its surplus for 2006-07 (July-June) to the Government which included an amount of Rs.34,309 crore on account of sale of SBI shareholding to the Government.

Excluding the transactions relating to transfer of the Reserve Bank's stake in the SBI to the Government, revenue receipts of the Central Government amounted to 26.7 per cent of the budget estimates (BE) in April-August 2007 as compared with 26.4 per cent in April-August 2006.

Tax revenue and non-tax revenue were 24.6 per cent and 36.8 per cent of the BE, respectively, during April-August 2007 as compared with 24.9 per cent and 32.9 per cent a year ago.

Total expenditure at 36.8 per cent of the BE in April-August 2007 was higher than 35.5 per cent a year ago. As a proportion to the BE, the gross fiscal deficit (GFD) and revenue deficit increased to 67.6 per cent and 122.9 per cent, respectively, during April-August 2007 as compared with 61.0 per cent and 93.7 per cent in the corresponding period last year. A notable feature of deficit financing this year so far has been the decline in net mobilisation from small savings deposits and certificates for the first time.

The gross market borrowings of the Central Government through dated securities at Rs.1,27,060 crore (Rs.1,17,548 crore a year ago) during 2007-08 so far (up to October 26, 2007) constituted 67.3 per cent of the BE. Net market borrowings at Rs.75,387 crore (Rs.65,951 crore a year ago) constituted 68.7 per cent of the BE. An additional amount of Rs.27,500 crore (net) was mobilised through issuance of Treasury Bills (TBs) over and above the rollover of TBs maturing during the period.

The weighted average yield and weighted average maturity of Central Government securities issued during 2007-08 so far (up to October 26, 2007) were higher at 8.20 per cent and 14.41 years, respectively, as compared with 7.91 per cent and 14.08 years for those issued during the corresponding period last year. As against the provisional net allocation of Rs.28,206 crore (gross Rs.45,385 crore) for their market borrowing programme, the State Governments have raised a net amount of Rs.8,808 crore up to October 26, 2007.

As in the past, an indicative issuance calendar for issue of dated securities for the second half of 2007-08 was issued on September 24, 2007 in consultation with the Central Government with a view to enabling institutional and retail investors to plan their investment in a better manner and also for providing transparency and stability in the Government securities market.

In addition to the market borrowing programme, recapitalisation bonds amounting to Rs.12,001 crore were issued in August and September, 2007. Moreover, special securities amounting to Rs.7,500 crore with features similar to securities issued to oil companies and the Food Corporation of India in 2006-07, would be issued during the remaining part of 2007-08.

Furthermore, it was announced on October 11, 2007 that the Central Government would bear 42.7 per cent (Rs.23,457 crore) of the total under-recoveries of the oil companies (estimated at Rs.54,935 crore for 2007-08) in the form of oil bonds. Thus, securities amounting to Rs.42,958 crore are planned to be issued by the Central Government (excluding MSS) in addition to the regular market borrowing programme for 2007-08 as against Rs.40,321 crore issued in 2006-07.

During the second quarter of 2007-08, financial markets remained generally stable with conditions of abundant liquidity. Reflecting this environment, interest rates moderated in almost all segments of the financial system. Overnight interest rates, which averaged 0.26 per cent in July, returned to the LAF corridor after the ceiling on reverse repo acceptance under the LAF was removed from August 6, 2007 and the CRR was increased from 6.5 per cent to 7.0 per cent with effect from the fortnight beginning August 4, 2007.

Despite the overall stability, transient spikes in overnight rates were witnessed in August. Call money rates averaged 6.31 per cent in August 2007. Some hardening of overnight rates was also witnessed in the second half of September on account of reduction in liquidity with the banking system due to sizeable tax outflows and build-up of the Centre's cash balances which was also reflected in reduced LAF reverse repo.

The call money rate has declined from 14.07 per cent in March 2007 to 6.31 per cent in August and to 6.01 per cent on October 26, 2007. Overnight rates in other segments, viz., market repo and collateralised borrowing and lending obligations (CBLO) have moved in tandem with call money rates.

Market repo (other than LAF) and CBLO rates declined from 8.13 and 7.73 per cent, respectively, in March 2007 to 5.66 and 6.00 per cent as on October 26, 2007. The daily average volume (one leg) in the call money market rose from Rs.11,608 crore in March 2007 to Rs.12,981 crore as on October 26, 2007. The corresponding volumes in the market repo were Rs.8,687 crore and Rs.27,075 crore, respectively. In the CBLO segment, the volumes were Rs.17,662 crore and Rs.25,090 crore, respectively. As on October 26, 2007 interest rates for CBLO, market repo and call money stood at 5.66 per cent, 6.00 per cent and 6.01 per cent, respectively.

The primary yield on 91-day Treasury Bills declined to 7.02 per cent on October 24, 2007 from 7.98 per cent on end-March 2007 whereas the yield on 364-day Treasury Bills declined to 7.36 per cent from 7.98 per cent over the same period.

There was higher mobilisation from CPs as the outstanding amount of CP was Rs.33,614 crore by end-September 2007 as compared with Rs.17,688 crore at end-March 2007, with the weighted average discount rate on CP declining to 8.95 per cent from 11.33 per cent over this period. In the market for certificates of deposit (CDs) also, the weighted average discount rate declined from 10.75 per cent at the end of March 2007 to

8.57 per cent by end-September, accompanied by an increase of 27.0 per cent in the outstanding amount (from Rs.93,272 crore to Rs.1,18,481 crore). It may be noted that overnight and short-term money market rates had firmed up at the end of March 2007 reflecting liquidity tightening resulting from end-year tax outflows.

In the foreign exchange market, large surplus conditions in the spot market resulted in a sharp increase in average daily turnover to US $ 52.9 billion in mid-September 2007 from a level of US $ 27.5 billion a year ago. While the inter-bank turnover increased from US $ 20 billion to US $ 37.6 billion, the merchant turnover increased from US $ 7 billion to US $ 15.2 billion. According to the triennial central bank survey conducted by the Bank for International Settlements (BIS), India is among the fastest growing foreign exchange markets in terms of turnover. There has been a general softening in forward premia across all maturities. The six-month forward premia eased from 3.60 per cent in March 2007 to 2.53 per cent by end-June 2007 and further to 1.20 per cent as on October 26, 2007.

The yield on Government securities with one-year residual maturity declined from 7.55 per cent at end-March 2007 to 7.40 per cent as on October 26, 2007. The yield on Government securities with 10-year residual maturity also declined from 7.97 per cent to 7.88 per cent. The yield on Government securities with 20-year residual maturity rose from 8.23 per cent to 8.28 per cent.

The yield spread between 10-year and one-year Government securities widened from 42 basis points to 48 basis points. The yield spread between 20-year and one-year Government securities also widened from 68 basis points to 88 basis points during the same period. 30. During April-October 2007, public sector banks (PSBs) decreased their deposit rates, particularly at the upper end of the range for various maturities, by 25-60 basis points.

Deposit rates of PSBs increased by 25-75 basis points at the lower end for deposits of maturities of one year and above. Interest rates offered by the PSBs on deposits of above one year maturity moved from 7.25-9.75 per cent in April 2007 to 8.0-9.5 per cent in October 2007.

Private sector banks' deposit rates for up to one year maturity decreased from a range of 3.00-10.00 per cent to 2.5-9.25 per cent over the same period. Foreign banks' deposit rates for up to one year maturity also declined from a range of 3.00-9.50 per cent to 2.00-9.00 per cent during the same period.

The benchmark prime lending rates (BPLRs) of private sector banks moved from a range of 12.50-17.25 per cent to 13.00-16.50 per cent in the same period. The range of BPLRs for PSBs and foreign banks, however, remained unchanged at 12.50-13.50 per cent and 10.00-15.50 per cent, respectively, during this period.

During the second quarter of 2007-08, equity market activity recorded a pick-up in terms of issuances in the domestic primary segment as well as in international stock exchanges.

The BSE Sensex (1978-79=100) increased from 13,072 at end-March 2007 to cross the 15,000 level on July 9, 2007, the 16,000 level on September 19, 2007, the 17,000 level on September 27, 2007, the 18,000 level on October 9, 2007, the 19,000 level on October 15, 2007 and closed at 19,243 on October 26, 2007.

According to the Securities and Exchange Board of India (SEBI), net investments by foreign institutional investors (FIIs) in the equity market were significantly higher at Rs.62,139 crore (US $ 15.1 billion) during April-October 19, 2007 as compared with net investments of Rs.10,231 crore (US $ 2.2 billion) in the corresponding period last year.

Mutual funds mobilised funds of the order of Rs.1,05,614 crore during April-September 2007 as against Rs.60,048 crore a year ago.

MACROECONOMIC AND MONETARY DEVELOPMENTS: THIRD QUARTER REVIEW 2006-07

The Reserve Bank of India on 29th January 2007 released the document "Macroeconomic and Monetary Developments: Third Quarter Review 2006-07" to serve as a backdrop to the Third Quarter Review of the Annual Statement on Monetary Policy for 2006-07 being announced on January 31, 2007.

The highlights of macroeconomic and monetary developments during 2006-07 so far are:

The Real Economy

The robust performance of the Indian economy continued during the second quarter (July-September) of 2006-07. According to the Central Statistical Organisation (CSO), real gross domestic product (GDP) growth accelerated to 9.2 per cent in the second quarter from 8.9 per cent in the preceding quarter and 8.4 per cent a year ago led by manufacturing and services.

With both the first and second quarters of 2006-07 recording higher growth over the corresponding quarters of 2005-06, real GDP growth accelerated to 9.1 per cent in the first half of 2006-07 from 8.5 per cent a year ago. Growth in agriculture and allied activities decelerated to 2.6 per cent during April-September 2006 from 3.7 per cent a year ago.

Industrial production continued its growth momentum during 2006-07, with growth accelerating to 10.6 per cent during April-November 2006 from 8.3 per cent a year ago. The manufacturing sector with double digit growth (11.5 per cent) continued to be the key driver of industrial activity, contributing almost 91.2 per cent of the growth in industry.

Growth in infrastructure industries improved to 7.8 per cent during April-November 2006 from 5.2 per cent during the same period of 2005 on account of better performance of electricity, crude petroleum and petroleum refinery products.

During the first half of 2006-07, growth in the services sector accelerated to 10.6 per cent from 10.2 per cent during the first half of 2005-06.

The industry and the services sectors have remained strong during 2006-07 so far. Business confidence surveys also suggest that economic activity is likely to remain buoyant in the near term.

The ongoing momentum in economic growth is, thus, likely to remain robust in the rest of 2006-07. Profits after tax of select non-Government non-financial companies increased by 49.4 per cent during the quarter ended September 2006 as compared with 34.7 per cent in the preceding quarter. Ratio of profits after tax to sales of select non-Government non-financial companies improved to 11.0 per cent during the quarter ended September 2006 from 10.6 per cent in the preceding quarter and 8.5 per cent a year ago.

Fiscal Situation

Central Government finances for the first eight months (April-November) of the fiscal year 2006-07 show that the fiscal deficit, as per cent of the full year budget estimate (BE), was placed lower than that in the corresponding period of the previous year. Revenue deficit, as per cent of BE, however, continued to be higher than in the previous year on account of increase in non-Plan expenditure which offset buoyant tax revenues. Contraction in non-defence capital outlay and loans and advances, however, moderated the impact on fiscal deficit.

Gross and net market borrowings (including dated securities and 364-day Treasury Bills) raised by the Centre during 2006-07 up to January 22, 2007 amounted to 83.1 per cent and 80.4 per cent of the budget estimates as compared with 84.9 per cent and 82.7 per cent, respectively, a year ago.

During 2006-07 so far (up to January 22, 2007), the States have raised market loans amounting to Rs.14,204 crore (or 54.9 per cent of gross allocation) exclusively through auctions.

The weekly average utilisation of WMA and overdraft by the States at Rs.256 crore during April-December 2006 was lower than that of Rs.639 crore in the corresponding period of 2005.

The cash surplus position of the State Governments has improved further during 2006-07 so far. This was reflected in an increase in their investments in 14-day Treasury Bills to Rs.41,567 crore (weekly average) during April-December 2006 from Rs.32,789 crore in the corresponding period of the previous year. The surplus cash balances of State Governments are automatically invested in 14-day Treasury Bills.

Monetary and Liquidity Conditions

Bank credit continued to grow at a strong pace during 2006-07. Non-food credit of scheduled commercial banks (SCBs) grew by 31.2 per cent (Rs. 4,07,735 crore), year-on-year (y-o-y), as on January 5, 2007, as compared with a similar 31.2 per cent (Rs. 3,11,013 crore) a year ago.

Sustained growth of bank credit could be accommodated by acceleration in deposit growth of SCBs of Rs. 4,38,037 crore (22.5 per cent) (y-o-y) as on January 5, 2007 from Rs. 2,85,182 crore (17.2 per cent) as on January 6, 2006.

Concomitantly, broad money growth has remained above the indicative trajectory. Broad money growth was Rs. 5,17,318 crore (20.4 per cent) (y-o-y) as on January 5, 2007 as compared with 3,50,747 crore (16.0 per cent) a year ago.

Banks' SLR investments, as a proportion of their net demand and time liabilities, declined further from their end-March 2006 levels.

The Reserve Bank continued to modulate market liquidity with the help of LAF repo and reverse repos and issuance of securities under the Market Stabilisation Scheme (MSS). Furthermore, the Reserve Bank raised the cash reserve ratio by

50 basis points in two phases with effect from the fortnight beginning December 23, 2006. Liquidity management emerged to be more complex during the past year, with greater variation in market liquidity, largely reflecting variations in cash balances of the Governments and capital flows.

Reserve money growth was Rs.1,06,846 crore (20.0 per cent) (y-o-y) as on January 19, 2007 as compared with Rs.69,213 crore (14.9 per cent) a year ago.

Price Situation

Headline inflation in major advanced economies eased during September-October 2006 on the back of base effects as well as the sharp decline in international crude oil prices, but again rose during November-December 2006; core inflation remains firm.

Many central banks such as the European Central Bank (ECB), the Bank of England, the Reserve Bank of Australia, and the South African Reserve Bank continued with pre-emptive monetary tightening to abate the second round effects.

In India, inflation movements in 2006-07 have been driven by primary food articles and manufactured products prices.

Headline inflation, based on movement in the wholesale price index (WPI), increased to 6.0 per cent as on January 13, 2007 from 4.1 per cent at end-March 2006 and 4.2 per cent a year ago. The y-o-y inflation, excluding the fuel group, at 6.6 per cent was above the headline inflation rate of 6.0 per cent as on January 13, 2007.

Consumer price inflation has remained higher than the WPI inflation since November 2005, reflecting the higher order of increase in food prices as well as the higher weight of food items in the CPI.

Consumer price inflation for industrial workers was placed at 6.3 per cent in November 2006 while that for urban non-manual employees, agricultural labourers and rural labourers was placed at 6.9 per cent, 8.9 per cent and 8.3 per cent, respectively, in December 2006.

Financial Markets

Short-term money rates remained generally within the reverse repo rate and repo rate corridor till mid-December 2006. However, since the last fortnight of December 2006, call rates moved up sharply.

In the foreign exchange market, the Indian rupee appreciated vis-à-vis the US dollar during the third quarter of 2006-07 (October-December 2006).

Yields on the longer maturity bonds in the Government securities market softened between during October-November 2006 but increased in December 2006 and January 2007.

Banks' deposit and lending rates edged up further during the third quarter (October-December 2006) in the wake of strong credit demand.

The External Economy

India's external sector has continued to register robust performance during 2006-07 so far.

Merchandise exports have exhibited strong growth, notwithstanding some deceleration (22.0 per cent during April-December 2006 as compared with 29.9 per cent a year ago). Non-oil imports recorded a deceleration mainly on account of decline in imports of gold and silver, and pearls, precious and semi-precious stones; imports of capital goods, however, remained buoyant. Growth in oil imports remained high on the back of higher volumes.

Sustained growth in exports of services and remittances continued to provide buoyancy to the surplus in the invisibles account, which enabled financing a large part of the deficit on the merchandise trade account.

The current account deficit widened from US $ 7.2 billion during April-September 2005 to US $ 11.7 billion during April-September 2006.

The higher current account deficit was easily financed by continuing large capital flows. Capital flows increased from US $ 13.7 billion during April-September 2005 to US $ 20.3 billion during April-September 2006, driven by FDI flows which nearly doubled to US $ 8.6 billion in April-November 2006 from a year ago.

Foreign exchange reserves have increased by US $ 26.5 billion during 2006-07 so far to US $ 178.1 billion as on January 19, 2007.

RBI INCREASES CASH RESERVE RATIO (CRR)

Reserve Bank of India has increased CRR of the scheduled commercial banks, regional rural banks (RRBs), scheduled state co-operative banks and scheduled primary (urban) co-operative banking system by one-half of one percentage point of their net demand and time liabilities (NDTL) in two stages, effective from specified fortnights as indicated below:

December 23, 2006- 5.25

January 06, 2007- 5.50

As a result of the above increases in CRR on liabilities to banking system, an amount of about Rs.13,500 crore of resources of banks would be absorbed. In view of the following significant developments, particularly on the domestic front, RBI has decided to increase CRR:

(a) Real GDP growth at 9.2 per cent during July-September 2006 and 9.1 per cent in the first half of 2006-07.

(b) Year-on-year increase in non-food bank credit up to November 24, 2006 was 30.1 per cent on top of an increase of 31.1 per cent a year ago.

(c) Year-on-year money supply (M3) growth at 19.4 per cent by November 24, 2006, up from 17.3 per cent a year ago.

(d) Year-on-year expansion in reserve money as on November 24, 2006 was 17.5 per cent, higher than 14.9 per cent a year ago.

(e) Additional liquidity amounting to Rs.12,342 crore was absorbed under the market stabilisation scheme (MSS) during 2006-07 up to November 2006. The balances under the MSS increased from Rs.29,000 crore on March 31, 2006 to Rs.39,233 crore by November 30, 2006.

(f) Year-on-year WPI inflation has risen from 4.1 per cent at end-March 2006 to 5.3 per cent as on November 25, 2006 higher than 4.5 per cent a year ago.

(g) Year-on-year inflation based on the consumer price index (CPI) for industrial workers, urban non-manual employees, agricultural labourers and rural labourers are 7.3 per cent, 7.2 per cent, 8.4 per cent and 8.1 per cent in October 2006 from 4.2 per cent, 4.6 per cent, 3.2 per cent and 3.2 per cent, respectively a year ago.

(h) As per the RBI's Industrial Outlook survey, a majority of respondents from the private corporate sector expect higher increase in prices of both inputs and outputs. There are reports of growing strains on domestic capacity utilisation. There are also reports that expansion of capacity is underway but the realisation could be constrained over the next two years.

However, the conditions in financial markets continue to be stable and orderly.

A seasonal decline in prices of food articles could moderate the inflation pressures but the WPI inflation excluding food articles is close to 5.0 per cent. The recent reduction in prices of petrol and diesel will moderate inflation, but the overall impact on inflation expectations requires to be monitored and moderated.

The external sector continues to be strong and current account deficit is likely to be close to the trend, and will continue to be accommodated by net capital flows. However, it is necessary to recognize the challenges emanating from capital flows and consequent impact on increasing liquidity.

11

Monetary and External Economy

INTRODUCTION

The growth in broad money (M3), year-on-year (y-o-y), was 21.6 per cent (Rs. 6,09,610 crore) on July 6, 2007 as compared with 19.0 per cent (Rs. 4,51,636 crore) a year ago. Aggregate deposits of banks, y-o-y, increased by 22.8 per cent (Rs. 5,42,766 crore) on July 6, 2007 as compared with 19.6 per cent (Rs. 3,90,409 crore) a year ago.

Growth in bank credit moderated after the strong pace in the preceding three years. Non-food credit by scheduled commercial banks (SCBs) moderated to 24.4 per cent (Rs.3,67,258 crore), y-o-y, as on July 6, 2007 from 32.8 per cent (Rs. 3,70,899 crore) a year ago.

Reserve money expanded by 29.1 per cent (21.7 per cent adjusted for the first round impact of the increase in the cash reserve ratio), y-o-y, as on July 20, 2007 as compared with 17.2 per cent a year ago.

Liquidity conditions continued to be influenced by movements in capital flows and cash balances of the Governments. The Reserve Bank modulated market liquidity with the help of issuances of securities under the Market Stabilisation Scheme (MSS), operations under Liquidity Adjustment Facility (LAF) and increase in the cash reserve ratio (CRR).

Price Situation

Both headline and core inflation in major economies have remained firm during 2007-08 so far, reflecting the combined impact of high commodity prices and strong demand conditions. Several central banks further tightened monetary policy during March-June 2007.

Global commodity prices firmed up further in the first quarter of 2007-08 led by crude oil, metals and edible oils. WTI crude oil prices increased to US $ 76 a barrel on July 19, 2007 from around US $ 60 a barrel in March 2007. The overall food price index compiled by the IMF increased by 10 per cent in June 2007 (y-o-y) on top of an increase of 12 per cent a year ago. Reflecting the sustained rise in food prices, the IMF's food price index in June 2007 reached its highest level since 1981.

In India, inflation based on the wholesale price index (WPI) initially rose to above 6.0 per cent in early April 2007 but eased to 4.4 per cent by July 14, 2007. Manufactured products inflation was 4.6 per cent on July 14, 2007 as compared with 3.9 per cent a year ago.

Consumer price inflation also eased somewhat to 6.1-7.5 per cent by June 2007 from 7.6-9.2 per cent in March 2007, though it continued to remain high, mainly reflecting the impact of higher food prices.

Pre-emptive monetary measures since mid-2004 accompanied by fiscal and supply-side measures helped in containing inflation.

Financial Markets

Indian financial markets remained generally orderly for the most part of the first quarter of 2007-08. Capital flows and swings in cash balances of the Governments were the main drivers of liquidity conditions in the financial markets, imparting volatility to overnight interest rates.

The call money rate softened during April-June 2007 and remained below the reverse repo rate on many occasions on the back of easier liquidity conditions. Interest rates in the collateralised segment of the overnight money market also softened and remained below the call rate during the quarter.

In the foreign exchange market, the Indian rupee appreciated vis-a-vis all major currencies (US dollar, Euro, Pound sterling and Japanese yen) during the first quarter.

Yields in the Government securities market, which hardened up to mid-June 2007 eased thereafter.

Banks' deposit and lending rates rose further during the first quarter; however, there was some softening in deposit rates in July 2007.

The External Economy

The merchandise trade deficit, on a balance of payments basis, rose from US $ 51.8 billion (6.4 per cent of GDP) in 2005-06 to US $ 64.9 billion (7.1 per cent of GDP) in 2006-07. Net invisibles increased from 5.3 per cent of GDP during 2005-06 to 6.0 per cent of GDP during 2006-07 and continued to finance a large part of the merchandise trade deficit.

The current account deficit, as a proportion to GDP, in 2006-07 was, thus, contained at the previous year's level of 1.1 per cent. Net of remittances, the current account deficit was 4.0 per cent of GDP in 2006-07 (4.1 per cent in 2005-06 and 3.3 per cent in 2004-05).

Net capital inflows were substantially higher than those in 2005-06 reflecting large flows under foreign direct investment (FDI) and external commercial borrowings. With capital flows (net) (US$ 46.2 billion) remaining well above the current account deficit (US$ 9.6 billion), the overall balance of payments recorded a surplus of US$ 36.6 billion during 2006-07, which was higher than US$ 15.1 billion recorded during 2005-06. During 2007-08 so far, merchandise exports and imports exhibited acceleration in growth.

Capital flows have remained buoyant led by FII inflows. During 2007-08 (up to July 13, 2007), FIIs registered net inflows of US $ 8.4 billion as compared with outflows of US $ 2.0 billion in the corresponding period of 2006-07. FDI inflows were US $ 1.6 billion during April 2007 (US $ 0.7 billion a year ago). Non-resident deposits registered net outflows amounting to US $ 274 million during April 2007 as against net inflows of US $ 253 million during April 2006.

India's foreign exchange reserves were US $ 222.0 billion as on July 20, 2007, an increase of US $ 22.9 billion over end-March 2007 level.

A comparison of major reserve holding countries over the period 2000-2006 shows that current account surpluses accounted for 179 per cent and 138 per cent of accretion to reserves in Japan and Russia, respectively, and 56 per cent each in case of China and Korea. In contrast, in India, over the same period, accretion to foreign exchange reserves was almost entirely due to capital inflows. Total reserves increased by US $ 143.8 billion during 2000-2006; net capital inflows increased by US $ 143.9 billion over the same period.

This Review consists of three sections:

The Reserve Bank of India on 30th July 2007 the document "Macroeconomic and Monetary Developments: First Quarter Review 2007-08" to serve as a backdrop to the First Quarter Review of the Annual Statement on Monetary Policy for 2007-08 announced on July 31, 2007.

The highlights of macroeconomic and monetary developments during 2007-08 are:

The Real Economy

The cumulative rainfall recorded during the 2007 monsoon (up to July 25) was 4 per cent above normal as compared with 14 per cent below normal a year ago. As on July 20, 2007, sowing was undertaken in almost 54 per cent of normal area under kharif crops. Total area sown was 1.7 per cent higher than that in the corresponding period of 2006.

Industrial production remained robust during April-May 2007, recording a year-on-year expansion of 11.7 per cent. The manufacturing sector remained the key driver of industrial activity with growth of 12.7 per cent.

The infrastructure sector recorded a higher growth of 8.1 per cent during April-May 2007 as compared with 7.2 per cent than a year ago mainly on account of improvement in electricity and petroleum refinery products.

Growth rates in tourist arrivals, revenue earning freight traffic of the railways, new cell phone connections, export cargo handled by civil aviation, passengers handled by civil aviation, cement and steel moderated. On the other hand, cargo handled at major ports accelerated vis-à-vis the previous year.

Fiscal Situation

Available information on Central Government finances for April-May 2007 indicates that all the key deficit indicators were lower than a year ago in absolute terms. As percentage of budget estimates, gross fiscal deficit was also lower than in April-May 2006. The improvement in Central Government finances during April-May 2007 was brought about by higher tax revenues, higher non-debt capital receipts and lower plan expenditure.

Gross and net market borrowings (including dated securities and 364-day Treasury Bills) of the Centre during 2007-08 (up to July 26, 2007) amounted to Rs.85,628 crore and Rs.46,047 crore, respectively, accounting for 45.3 per cent and 42.0 per cent, respectively, of the estimated borrowings for the year. During the corresponding period of the previous year, the gross and net borrowings accounted for 39.5 per cent and 31.3 per cent, respectively, of the actual borrowings for 2006-07.

During 2007-08 (up to July 26, 2007), the Centre took recourse to WMA for 72 days as compared with 33 days during the same period in 2006-07.

During 2007-08 (up to July 26, 2007), fourteen States have raised market borrowings amounting to Rs. 8,542 crore (25.6 per cent of gross allocation for the year). The average utilisation of WMA and overdraft by the States was Rs.694 crore during 2007-08 (up to July 20, 2007) as compared with Rs. 258 crore in the corresponding period of the previous year. The average investments by the States in Treasury Bills during April-June 2007 amounted to Rs.68,800 crore as against Rs. 52,876 crore during the corresponding period of the previous year.

FIRST QUARTER REVIEW OF ANNUAL MONETARY POLICY FOR THE YEAR 2007-08

1. Assessment of Macroeconomic and Monetary Developments Domestic Developments
2. At the end of May 2007, the Central Statistical Organisation (CSO) released quarterly real GDP growth estimates for January-March 2007 at 9.1 per cent as against 10.0 per cent a year ago. Along with revisions for the preceding three quarters, real GDP growth in 2006-07 was raised to 9.4 per cent from 9.2 per cent in the CSO's February 2007 advance estimates. In the revised estimates, real GDP originating in agriculture, industry and services sectors increased by 2.7 per cent, 11.0 per cent and 11.0 per cent, respectively, in 2006-07 as against 6.0 per cent, 8.0 per cent and 10.3 per cent in 2005-06. Over the four-year period starting in 2003-04 when the current expansionary phase began, real GDP growth has averaged 8.6 per cent, up from 5.1 per cent in the preceding four years and also above the average of 5.7 per cent achieved in the 1990s.
3. The progress of the 2007 south-west monsoon season has been satisfactory so far, despite initial delays in its

onset over the western, north-western and central regions. Of the normal area of 71.9 million hectares under kharif foodgrain crops, 30.1 million hectares were covered by sowing by July 20 this year, which is comparable with 30.0 million hectares in the corresponding period of the preceding year. Also, 12.2 million hectares were covered under major oilseeds as against 11.7 million hectares last year. While area sown under cotton (7.2 million hectares) was higher, that under sugarcane (4.4 million hectares) and jute (0.8 million hectares) was somewhat lower as compared with the previous year. During June 1 to July 25, 2007 rainfall has been 4 per cent above the long-period average (LPA) and excess/normal in 29 of the 36 meteorological subdivisions, according to the India Meteorological Department (IMD). The IMD has updated its initial forecast released on April 19, 2007 and has placed the rainfall for the south-west monsoon season at 93 per cent of the LPA for the country as a whole in its latest forecast released on June 29, 2007.

4. The general index of industrial production (IIP) rose by 11.7 per cent in April-May 2007 from 10.8 per cent a year ago. The acceleration in industrial activity in the current financial year was led by manufacturing output which rose by 12.7 per cent as against 12.2 per cent in April-May 2006. Electricity generation and mining activity increased by 9.0 per cent and 3.0 per cent, respectively, as against 5.5 per cent and 3.2 per cent a year ago. Within manufacturing, industries such as machinery and equipment, food products, basic metals and alloys and chemicals emerged as growth drivers in 2007-08 (up to May). In terms of the use-based classification, production of capital goods increased by 18.6 per cent (20.6 per cent a year ago), while the

production of basic goods and intermediate goods rose by 9.4 per cent (9.2 per cent) and 10.5 per cent (10.5 per cent), respectively. Consumer goods output increased by 12.7 per cent (9.7 per cent). The six infrastructure industries, comprising nearly 27 per cent of the IIP, posted a growth of 8.1 per cent during April-May 2007 as against 7.2 per cent a year ago. Output growth picked up in respect of petroleum products and electricity, whereas some deceleration was recorded in steel, coal and cement output and crude petroleum production declined marginally.

5. Private corporate activity has gained strength and resilience, extending an unprecedented run of high growth that began in late 2002-03. Full information on corporate sector performance in 2006-07 that is now available for select private non-financial companies indicates that sales growth was of the order of 26.2 per cent, the highest since the 1980s. The pick-up in activity in 2006-07 was aided by improvements in operational efficiency, increased plant automation, cost control through better product mix, capacity utilisation and economies of scale, rising incomes from financial activity and return of pricing power. The growth in net profits of these companies was also high at 45.2 per cent as compared with 24.2 per cent a year ago. Over the period 2003-07, annual sales growth of select private non-financial companies averaged 20.8 per cent, while annual growth in net profits of these companies was 45.1 per cent. Early results for the first quarter of 2007-08 present a complex picture. Demand and investment conditions continue to be favourable. There is some deceleration in sales and profit growth, relative to the levels recorded in the preceding year. This may be reflecting some increase in input and staff costs.

6. In the Reserve Bank's Industrial Outlook Survey conducted during May 2007, nearly 60 per cent of respondent companies reported no change in capacity utilisation and a majority also indicated no change in the financial situation, working capital finance requirements and availability of finance. Responses relating to export orders, imports and profits were somewhat mixed. The business expectations index for April-June 2007 declined by 7.1 percentage points from its level in the preceding quarter and by 6.0 percentage points from its level a year ago. The outlook for July-September 2007 appears to be optimistic with 54 per cent of the respondents expecting an improvement in the overall business situation on the back of increase in production, order books and capacity utilisation. As in April-June 2007 a majority of respondents expect no change in the financial situation, working capital finance requirements, availability of finance and in profit margins. The overall business expectations index for July-September 2007 declined by 3.8 percentage points from its level in the previous quarter and by 5.4 percentage points from a year ago.
7. Business sentiment polled by other surveys presents a varied response, with optimism relating to sales volume, order books and net profits being tempered by the impact of exchange rate changes on services sector companies as well as export industries with relatively low import content. According to one survey, business confidence for July 2007 continues to be high but has declined by 8.8 per cent from its level in April-June 2007 and by 2.7 per cent year-on-year. Seasonally adjusted purchasing managers' indices for the first quarter of 2007-08 indicate favourable operating conditions in the manufacturing sector with the growth of output and

new orders being maintained, a modest rise in staff hiring and selling prices, some easing of input price inflation and a build-up in pre-production and finished goods inventory levels. These indices also reflect some optimism about the general business scenario among micro, small and medium enterprises with more than 90 per cent planning higher capital investment.

8. Services sector activity has expanded in the first quarter of 2007-08 as reflected in lead indicators. The communication sector has recorded robust growth with 8,18,000 new lines being added to the switching capacity of telephone exchanges and total telephone connections (fixed plus cellular) registering an increase of 77.6 per cent in April-May 2007 on a year-on-year basis. In the transport sector, cargo handled at major ports increased by 17.8 per cent, whereas railway revenue earnings from freight traffic increased by 6.0 per cent. In civil aviation, handling of import cargo and export cargo increased by 21.7 per cent and 1.6 per cent, respectively. Passengers handled at domestic and international terminals increased by 24.4 per cent and 13.1 per cent, respectively, as against 47.2 per cent and 14.1 per cent a year ago.

9. The CSO's end-May 2007 release provides estimates of expenditure components of GDP in 2006-07, which contain information on the evolution of the constituents of aggregate demand. As a proportion to GDP, real private final consumption expenditure declined to 57.2 per cent during 2006-07 from 58.9 per cent in the previous year. On the other hand, real gross fixed capital formation (GFCF) increased to 27.9 per cent of GDP from 26.7 per cent, indicating that the acceleration of growth in the Indian economy is mainly investment-driven, despite domestic private consumption remaining

the major component of aggregate demand. As regards external demand, net exports at (-) 2.8 per cent of GDP in 2006-07 were comparable to (-) 3.0 per cent in the previous year. Over the four-year period from 2003-04 to 2006-07, private consumption and gross capital formation increased in real terms by 6.3 per cent and 16.3 per cent per annum, respectively.

10. Turning to monetary and financial conditions, the year-on-year non-food credit growth of scheduled commercial banks (SCBs) at 24.4 per cent (Rs.3,67,258 crore) on July 6, 2007 was lower than 32.8 per cent (Rs.3,70,899 crore) a year ago. On a financial year basis, non-food credit declined by Rs.12,094 crore (0.6 per cent) during 2007-08 (up to July 6, 2007), in contrast to an increase of Rs.36,654 crore (2.5 per cent) in the corresponding period of the previous year. Food credit registered a decline of Rs.2,292 crore as against a decline of Rs.2,837 crore in the corresponding period last year.

11. Provisional information on the sectoral pattern of bank credit available up to March 2007 indicates some rebalancing of credit deployment, particularly in January-March 2007. During 2006-07, bank credit to agriculture recorded the highest growth (32.4 per cent), followed by the services sector (31.0 per cent), personal loans (26.5 per cent) and industry (25.7 per cent). Growth in housing and real estate loans decelerated modestly to 24.6 per cent and 69.8 per cent, respectively, although continuing to remain at elevated levels. Incremental credit off-take, however, was the highest in respect of industry (36.1 per cent), followed by services (25.2 per cent), personal loans (24.3 per cent) and agriculture (14.4 per cent). Within the industrial sector, sizeable credit off-take was recorded in respect of infrastructure (26.8 per cent), textiles (34.2 per cent), basic metals and

metal products (26.7 per cent), petroleum (41.0 per cent), food processing (27.9 per cent), engineering (24.5 per cent), chemicals (14.2 per cent) and construction (46.7 per cent). The share of textiles, infrastructure and basic metal and metal products in total credit to industry increased marginally from 10.6 per cent, 20.5 per cent and 12.0 per cent, respectively, to 11.3 per cent, 20.7 per cent and 12.1 per cent, while the share of engineering remained stable at 6.3 per cent. The share of industrial credit to chemicals declined from 8.8 per cent to 8.0 per cent. Priority sector advances grew by 24.0 per cent with a reduction in their share in outstanding non-food gross bank credit to 35.2 per cent in March 2007 from 36.4 per cent a year ago. Provisional information for May 2007 indicates continuing high credit growth to agriculture and the industrial sector and deceleration in credit to housing, real estate and personal loans.

12. On a year-on-year basis, commercial banks' investments in shares, bonds/debentures and commercial paper (CP) declined by Rs.809 crore (1.0 per cent) as compared with a decline of Rs.9,961 crore (11.1 per cent) a year ago. On a financial year basis, such investments by banks fell by Rs.4,145 crore (5.2 per cent) during 2007-08 so far (up to July 6), as against an increase of Rs.593 crore (0.7 per cent) in the corresponding period of 2006-07. Banks, however, invested Rs.45,048 crore in instruments issued by mutual funds as against only Rs.15,902 crore in the corresponding period of 2006-07. The year-on-year growth in total flow of resources from SCBs to the commercial sector was 23.1 per cent (Rs.3,66,450 crore), lower than 29.5 per cent (Rs.3,60,938 crore) a year ago.

13. The year-on-year increase in aggregate deposits of SCBs at 24.4 per cent (Rs.5,31,881 crore) up to July 6, 2007 was

higher than 20.9 per cent (Rs.3,77, 392 crore) a year ago. The outflow of long-term deposits during the preceding two years has been arrested and there were fresh accretions to long-term deposits in April-June 2007 which augurs well for banks' asset-liability management. On a financial year basis, aggregate deposits increased by Rs.1,05,534 crore (4.0 per cent) during 2007-08 up to July 6, 2007 as against an increase of Rs.72,913 crore (3.5 per cent) in the corresponding period of the previous year. The accretion to bank deposits during the current financial year so far (April-July 6, 2007) is at a 14-year high. The incremental annual non-food credit-deposit ratio as on July 6, 2007 declined to 69.0 per cent from 98.3 per cent a year ago.

14. By the beginning of the current financial year, several banks had drawn down holdings of statutory liquidity ratio (SLR)-eligible securities close to the statutory floor to accommodate the sustained non-food credit demand over the last three years. Reflecting the ongoing shifts in banks' portfolios to comply with the statutory requirements in view of this depletion, investment in Government and other approved securities by SCBs increased by Rs.59,515 crore during the current year so far (up to July 6, 2007) as against an increase of Rs.51,776 crore in the corresponding period of 2006-07. Exclusive of liquidity adjustment facility (LAF) operations, however, banks' investments in Government and other approved securities increased by Rs.27,331 crore as compared with an increase of Rs.751 crore a year ago. On July 6, 2007 commercial banks' holdings of Government and other approved securities was 28.7 per cent of the banking system's net demand and time liabilities (NDTL) as against 28.0 per cent at end-March 2007 and 31.5 per cent a year ago. Such investments

were Rs.1,10,207 crore above the statutory minimum of 25 per cent of NDTL. It may be recalled that the Union Budget, 2006-07 announced the unwinding of the entire outstanding amount of recapitalisation bonds/special securities of Rs.20,809 crore issued to nationalised banks. Accordingly, bonds/securities issued to 19 nationalised banks worth Rs.8,709 crore were converted into marketable securities on February 15, 2007 and made eligible for SLR purposes. This conversion augmented the stock of SLR-eligible securities in the system which would increase even further with the conversion of the remaining recapitalisation bonds/special securities during the course of 2007-08.

15. Money supply (M3) increased by 21.6 per cent on a year-on-year basis on July 6, 2007 which was above the projected trajectory of 17.0-17.5 per cent indicated in the Annual Policy Statement for 2007-08 and higher than 19.0 per cent a year ago. On a financial year basis, M3 increased by 3.8 per cent (Rs.1,24,365 crore) during 2007-08 up to July 6, 2007 as compared with the increase of 3.5 per cent (Rs.95,488 crore) in the corresponding period of the previous year.

16. Reserve money increased by 29.1 per cent on a year-on-year basis on July 20, 2007 which was higher than 17.2 per cent a year ago. During the current financial year up to July 20, 2007 reserve money increased by 6.2 per cent (Rs.43,659 crore) as compared with the increase of 1.8 per cent (Rs.10,069 crore) in the corresponding period of the previous year. Among the components, currency in circulation increased by 2.1 per cent (Rs.10,380 crore) as compared with 4.6 per cent (Rs.19,630 crore). Among the sources of reserve money, the Reserve Bank's net foreign currency assets increased by Rs.29,653 crore as against an increase of Rs.85,084

crore in the corresponding period last year. Adjusted for revaluation effects, the Reserve Bank's net foreign currency assets increased by Rs.72,947 crore as against an increase of Rs.30,663 crore in the corresponding period of 2006-07. Net Reserve Bank credit to the Central Government increased by Rs.18,875 crore as against a decline of Rs.6,356 crore.

17. Over the first quarter of 2007-08, generally easy conditions of liquidity were interspersed with sporadic and transient periods of tightness. Build-up of the Central Government's cash balances by the third week of March 2007 and balance sheet adjustments by banks at the end of March necessitated daily injections of liquidity through the LAF between March 16 and April 8. With the two-stage 50 basis point increase in the CRR announced on March 30 becoming effective on April 14 and April 28, repo operations were conducted again through April 16 - May 6. Throughout this period, contrastingly, market participants took recourse to reverse repos on a daily basis within the ceiling of Rs.3,000 crore set since March 5, 2007. During the quarter, an amount of Rs.18,377 crore was sterilised through the Market Stabilisation Scheme (MSS), warranted by strong capital inflows. By April 27, 2007 the Central Government slipped into drawal of ways and means advances (WMA) which deteriorated into overdraft during May 30-June 8. Call rates remained high during most part of April and May and ruled above the LAF repo rate.

18. From May 28, 2007 the system shifted into a phase of large surplus liquidity with continuous reverse repos on a daily basis, capped at Rs.3,000 crore, except on June 28-29, 2007 when the Reserve Bank injected money through repos to assuage liquidity tightness due to

advance tax outflows. While the Central Government vacated overdrafts from June 9, it continued to avail of WMA until June 17, 2007. There was a brief return to surplus cash balances during June 18-28 but recourse to WMA resumed thereafter, turning into overdrafts during July 3-8 and July 18, 2007 onwards. Additional market borrowings beyond the calendar were resorted to in order to finance, in part, the purchase of the Reserve Bank's stake in the State Bank of India. The amount of Rs.35,351 crore has been received by the Reserve Bank on June 29, 2007. The customary surplus transferable to the Central Government from the Reserve Bank for the year ending June 2007 is likely to be credited to the account of the Central Government in mid-August 2007.

19. The suffusion of liquidity flows in the financial markets mainly on account of the sharp depletion of the Central Government's cash balances was reflected in call rates plunging to close to one per cent levels, going even below on several occasions. The total overhang of liquidity under the LAF, the MSS and cash balances of the Central Government taken together declined from an average of Rs.97,449 crore in March 2007 to Rs.72,823 crore on July 27, 2007. An assessment of the total liquidity overhang, however, should also account for the transfer of Rs.35,351 crore from the Central Government to the Reserve Bank during this period. It also needs to be noted that in view of the ceiling on daily LAF reverse repos, the overhang as defined here provides the magnitude of liquidity impounded only through these instruments and it captures the overhang only when the Reserve Bank injects liquidity under the LAF. On a net basis, average daily LAF repos declined from Rs.11,858 crore in March 2007 to average daily

reverse repo of Rs.2,117 crore in July 2007 (up to July 27, 2007). The outstanding balances under MSS increased from Rs.64,863 crore at end-March 2007 to Rs.90,030 crore on July 27. Cash balances of the Centre with the Reserve Bank declined from an average of Rs.55,893 crore in March 2007 to a debit of Rs.20,199 crore on July 27, 2007.

20. Inflation, measured by variations in the wholesale price index (WPI) on a year-on-year basis, declined from 5.9 per cent at end-March 2007 to 4.4 per cent as on July 14, 2007. Prices of primary articles and manufactured products rose by 10.0 per cent and 4.6 per cent, respectively, as against the increase of 3.8 per cent and 3.9 per cent a year ago. Prices of the fuel group declined by 1.4 per cent as against an increase of 7.2 per cent a year ago. On an annual average basis, WPI inflation was 5.5 per cent up to July 14, 2007 as against 4.3 per cent a year ago.

21. Inflationary pressures emerging from supply constraints in the agricultural sector eased somewhat in the first quarter of 2007-08. The total stock of foodgrains with public agencies increased to 25.1 million tonnes on May 1, 2007 as against the buffer stock norm of 16.2 million tonnes and was also higher than 22.8 million tonnes a year ago. Year-on-year inflation in terms of foodgrains prices decelerated from 13.5 per cent in mid-December 2006 to 7.4 per cent by mid-July 2007. There has, however, been hardening in the prices of oilseeds since November 2006 with second-round effects on prices of edible oils and oil cakes. These three items, which together have a weight of 6.8 per cent in the WPI, contributed 28.7 per cent of headline inflation as on July 14, 2007. The easing of inflation in terms of prices of manufactures since end-March 2007 from 6.1 per cent

to 4.6 per cent by the second week of July has been mainly on account of decline in the prices of sugar and some deceleration in prices of basic metals and alloys and textiles.

22. The recent surge in global prices of several agricultural commodities is attributed partly to transitory factors such as drought-related supply shortfalls and low stocks. Weather-related setbacks to production occurred in a number of countries such as the US, the EU, Canada, Russia, Ukraine and most notably in Australia, where production fell by more than 50 per cent in 2006-07. According to the projections made by the Organisation for Economic Co-operation and Development (OECD)-Food and Agricultural Organisation (FAO), global prices of agricultural commodities are likely to rule higher than their historic equilibrium levels over the next ten years on account of various factors including the rapidly expanding bio-fuel industry which is pushing up the prices of agricultural commodities through spill-over effects. Growing cereal use for ethanol has caused reduction in acreage of oilseeds, particularly in the US, in favour of maize with adverse price effects. Indirectly, the prices of livestock products have also gone up due to rising feed costs. These developments have major implications for India to the extent of dependence on imports of edible oils and wheat for meeting domestic shortfalls.

23. The global dairy market has been facing an increasing demand for premium products which is likely to continue over the near-term. In Asia, particularly in China, and in Latin America, demand for milk products has gone up rapidly. US milk prices increased by 20 per cent during March-June 2007 fuelled by export demand and drought-related supply disruptions in Australia

and New Zealand. Milk futures in the Chicago Mercantile Exchange have risen by 60 per cent. The US Department of Agriculture expects milk prices to remain firm over the rest of 2007 and in 2008 as well. In India, milk prices reflected in the WPI increased by 7.7 per cent as on July 14, 2007, on a year-on-year basis, contributing 7.2 per cent to the headline WPI inflation.

24. Notwithstanding the higher production of foodgrains expected during 2006-07, there is a need for regular stock-taking, assessment and planning for ensuring the adequate availability of essential food articles in view of the global outlook. A comprehensive approach in this regard may take cognisance of changes in population, consumption patterns and the evolving trends in international trade.

25. During 2007-08 so far, West Texas Intermediate (WTI) prices have moved in a range of US $ 61-77 per barrel with UK Brent prices above the WTI by US $ 4.1 per barrel, while the premium of the WTI over the Dubai variety was US $ 1.40 per barrel. In tandem with the hardening of international crude prices, the average price of the Indian crude basket increased from US $ 56.2 per barrel in January-March 2007 to US $ 66.2 per barrel in April-June and to around US $ 73.5 per barrel on July 27, 2007, i.e., an increase of 32.9 per cent over the level in February 2007. Domestic prices of petrol and diesel have, however, remained unchanged since mid-February; prices of aviation turbine fuel, which are market-determined, have increased by 11.3 per cent in the same period. Excluding the fuel group, year-on-year inflation was 6.1 per cent on July 14, 2007 and was higher than headline inflation. According to the US Energy Information Administration (EIA), global demand is expected to increase by 1.3 million barrels

a day during 2007, while the supply is likely to increase only by 0.6 million barrels a day. WTI prices are expected to average US $ 65.7 per barrel in 2007.

26. On a year-on-year basis, inflation based on the consumer price index (CPI) for agricultural labourers and rural labourers increased to 7.8 per cent and 7.5 per cent, respectively, in June 2007 from 7.2 per cent each a year ago. Year-on-year inflation based on CPI for industrial workers and urban non-manual employees was placed at 6.6 per cent and 6.1 per cent, respectively, in May and June 2007 as against 6.3 per cent and 6.5 per cent, a year ago. The softening of food prices is being reflected in a reduced difference between inflation rates based on the CPI and the WPI.

27. In terms of proportions to budget estimates (BE), revenue receipts of the Central Government increased to 5.3 per cent during April-May 2007 from 4.8 per cent in April-May 2006. Total expenditure at 13.3 per cent was lower than 16.3 per cent a year ago. Both Plan and non-Plan expenditures were lower as proportions to BE than a year ago. Accordingly, the gross fiscal deficit (GFD) declined to 41.2 per cent from 48.5 per cent a year ago. The revenue deficit at 83.0 per cent of the BE in April-May 2007 was marginally higher than 81.0 per cent in the corresponding period last year.

28. Gross market borrowings (dated securities and 364-day Treasury Bills) of the Central Government during 2007-08 at Rs.85,628 crore up to July 27, 2007 (Rs.70,813 crore a year ago) constituted 45.4 per cent of the BE while net market borrowings at Rs.46,047 crore (Rs.34,822 crore) constituted 42.0 per cent of the BE. Additional borrowings of Rs.6,000 crore through 182-day Treasury Bills and Rs.18,500 crore through 91-day Treasury Bills

were undertaken in June 2007 in order to, inter alia, support the special operation of funding the transfer of the Reserve Bank's stake in the State Bank of India to the Government of India. Against the allocated net borrowing programme of Rs.23,359 crore for 2007-08, State Governments have raised a net amount of (-) Rs.645 crore (gross Rs. 8,541 crore; repayment: Rs.9,186 crore) during the current year (up to July 27, 2007).

29. During the first quarter of 2007-08, financial markets experienced sizeable fluctuations in liquidity and attendant episodes of volatility. Call money rates stayed firm during most part of April and May 2007, due to the usual tightening of liquidity at the end of March 2007 which were accentuated by CRR increases referred to earlier. Call rates stayed above the LAF corridor for prolonged periods with intermittent fluctuations. In June, market conditions shifted into surplus liquidity, engendered by large drawdown of the Central Government's cash balances during end-May and early June and capital inflows. Call rates hovered around one per cent for most part of June and July (up to July 27) except on June 28-29, 2007 when advance tax outflows briefly pushed up call rates above the LAF repo rate. Overnight rates in the call, market repo and collateralised borrowing and lending obligations (CBLO) segments have displayed close co-movement. The interest rate in the call market declined from an average of 14.07 per cent in March 2007 to 8.33 per cent, 6.96 per cent and 2.42 per cent in April, May and June 2007 and further to 0.90 per cent in July 2007. Interest rates in the market repo (outside the LAF) and CBLO segments declined from 8.13 per cent and 7.73 per cent, respectively, in March 2007 to 6.76 per cent and 6.12 per cent in April 2007 and further to 0.26 per cent and 0.07

per cent in July 2007. The daily average volume (one leg) in the call money market declined from Rs.11,608 crore in March 2007 to Rs.8,687 crore in July 2007. The corresponding volumes in the market repo were Rs.8,646 crore and Rs.12,070 crore, respectively, whereas in the CBLO segment, the volumes were Rs.17,662 crore and Rs.18,509 crore, respectively. As on July 27, 2007 the weighted average interest rate for CBLO, market repo and call rate stood at 0.02 per cent, 0.18 per cent and 0.22 per cent, respectively.

30. In the primary market, the yield on 91-day Treasury Bills declined from 7.97 per cent at end-March 2007 to 4.46 per cent by July 25, 2007. The yield on 364-day Treasury Bills also recorded a decline from 7.98 per cent to 6.58 per cent by July 18, 2007. There was a marked increase in commercial paper (CP) issuances and the outstanding amount increased to Rs.26,256 crore by end-June 2007 from Rs.17,688 crore at end-March 2007. The weighted average discount rate on CP declined from 11.33 per cent to 8.93 per cent over this period.

    In the market for certificates of deposit (CDs), the weighted average discount rate declined from 10.75 per cent at the end of March 2007 to 9.37 per cent by end-June and the outstanding amount increased from Rs.93,272 crore to Rs.98,337 crore over this period.

31. In the secondary market, the yield on government securities with one-year residual maturity moved down from 7.55 per cent at end-March 2007 to 6.84 per cent by July 27, 2007. The yields on Government securities with 10-year and 20-year residual maturity also eased during this period from 7.97 per cent to 7.89 per cent and from 8.23 per cent to 8.21 per cent, respectively. Consequently, the yield spread between 10-year and one-year Government securities widened from 42 basis

points to 105 basis points whereas the spread between 20-year and one-year Government securities widened from 68 basis points to 137 basis points over this period.

32. Banks had generally increased their deposit rates by about 25-50 basis points across various maturities between March 2007 and June 2007, but reduced them during July 2007, especially in the shorter maturities. The majority of public sector banks (PSBs) adjusted their deposit rates upwards by 10-25 basis points on maturities above one year, particularly at the longer end. Interest rates offered by the PSBs on deposits of above one-year maturity moved up from 7.25-9.50 per cent in March 2007 to 7.25-9.60 per cent in July 2007. Private sector banks' deposit rates for one year and up to three years maturity moved from 6.75-9.75 per cent in March 2007 to 6.75-10.25 per cent in July 2007, while interest rates on deposits greater than three years maturity increased from 7.75-9.60 per cent to 7.50-10.00 per cent over the same period. The range of interest rates offered by foreign banks on deposits of maturities above one year remained largely unchanged at 2.50-9.50 per cent in July 2007 compared to 3.50-9.50 per cent in March 2007. The benchmark prime lending rates (BPLRs) of PSBs and private sector banks moved from a range of 12.25-12.75 per cent and 12.00-16.50 per cent to 12.50-13.50 per cent and 13.00-17.25 per cent, respectively, in the same period. The range of BPLRs for foreign banks was 10.00-15.50 per cent during the period.

33. In the foreign exchange market, large surplus conditions in the spot market were accompanied by a sharp increase in average daily turnover in the foreign exchange market to US $ 38.2 billion from a level of US $ 23.6 billion a year ago. While the inter-bank turnover increased from

US $ 17.1 billion to US $ 27.7 billion, the merchant turnover increased from US $ 6.5 billion to US $ 10.5 billion. Forward premia spiked in April 2007 but in subsequent months, there has been a softening across all maturities. The six-month forward premia eased from 3.60 per cent in March 2007 to 2.53 per cent by end-June 2007 and further to 1.28 per cent as on July 27, 2007.

34. The equity markets were buoyant on the back of strong corporate profitability, a positive investment climate and sound fundamentals. The BSE Sensex (1978-79=100) increased from 13,072 at end-March 2007 to cross the 15,000 level on July 9, 2007 and reached 15,795 on July 24, 2007. On July 27, 2007 the BSE Sensex declined to 15,235.

RECENT MACROECONOMIC DEVELOPMENTS AND THE BANKING SYSTEM

For a greater part of the twentieth century, the role of the financial system was perceived as mobilising the massive resource requirements for growth. Since the 1970s and 1980s, development economics underwent a paradigm shift. The financial system is no longer viewed as a passive mobiliser of funds. Efficiency in financial intermediation i.e., the ability of financial institutions to intermediate between savers and investors, to set economic prices for capital and to allocate resources among competing demands is now emphasised. Developments in endogenous growth theory since the late 1980s indicate that efficiency in financial intermediation is a source of technical progress to be exploited for generating increasing returns and sustaining high growth. These changes have provided the rationale for many developing countries to undertake wide-ranging reforms of their financial systems so as to prepare them for their true resource allocation function. As important financial inte rmediaries, banks have a special role to play in this new dispensation.

The sharp downturn in global macroeconomic prospects and the continuing sluggishness in domestic industrial activity have necessitated a revision in the forecast for India's real GDP growth in 2001-02 from 6.0-6.5 per cent expected at the time of the April 2001 Monetary and Credit Policy Statement to 5.0-6.0 per cent in the mid-term review of the policy. The downward revision is primarily predicated on the outlook for the industrial sector which grew by barely 2.2 per cent in April-October 2001 as against 5.9 per cent in the corresponding period of last year, mainly on account of the slowdown in manufacturing and mining and quarrying. Capital goods production declined by as much as 6.6 per cent and several sectors recorded a slow down in growth rate or an absolute decline. On the other hand, agriculture sector, supported by reasonable monsoon, recorded a rebound in growth. The kharif output is expected to cross a new peak of 105.6 million tonnes and prospects for the rabi crop are also good. On the external front, merchandise exports increased marginally by 0.5 per cent in the first eight months of 2001-02. While oil imports fell by 13.4 per cent, the non-oil imports showed an increase of 8.4 per cent. Despite a moderate widening of the trade deficit, continuing buoyancy in net invisible receipts has kept the current account deficit very low. According to available data, net capital flows are also likely to be of a higher order than in the preceding year. Foreign exchange reserves rose to US $ 48.0 billion as on December 28, 2001 recording an accretion of the order of the US $ 5.8 billion over the end-March 2001 level.

In the context of the recent deceleration in the economy the intermediation role assumes even greater relevance. Banks and financial institutions should endeavour to play a 'supply-leading' rather than 'demand-following' role in initiating the upturn by energising the financial intermediation process. By virtue of a bird's eye view of the economy and their superior credit assessment of the investment proposals and the efficiency of capital, banks should endeavour to economise on 'search' costs in identifying and nurturing growth impulses in the commodity and service producing sectors of the economy.

In the recent period, monetary policy in India has also moved into a counter-cyclical stance signalled by cuts in key interest rates and cash reserve requirements. At the same time, market operations have ensured adequate liquidity to support the revival of aggregate demand with a clear preference for softening of interest rates within the overall institutional constraints on the interest rate regime. Inflation has been steadily falling and this has had a positive impact on inflation expectations, along with the underlying resilience of the macroeconomic fundamentals of the Indian economy. The 50 basis point reduction in the Bank Rate and the 200 basis point reduction in the CRR, announced recently, are expected to significantly enhance the lendable resources of the banking system.

The current situation of comfortable liquidity provides an opportunity for banks to transform idle liquidity into investible resources for growth. The easy interest rate environment would make it possible for banks to 'price in' projects which would have earlier remained unfunded due to inherently lower returns to capital or due to lack of access to prime lending rates. This will, however, require reassessment of portfolios and internal liquidity constraints, even adjustments in risk profiles and risk management. The deceleration in the industrial growth scenario, of course, opens up the moral hazard of adverse selection and the possibilities of large-scale contamination of portfolios. In a situation of generalised slowdown, unviable projects can look potentially bankable given the scarcity of investment avenues.

Nevertheless, the possibilities for financial intermediation in the current situation are too varied and challenging to ignore. There is no systematic evidence that financial sector reforms by themselves and without supportive policies in other areas, can contribute to a revival of the economy; yet this is a time when the responsibility on the financial system to contribute to the process of economic revival is greater than before. Periods of downturn in economic activity also provide opportunities for banks to undertake consolidation and strengthening. There is a strong complementarity between financial stability and macroeconomic stability. The interests of both are served by a stable and resilient financial system.

In recent years, various measures have been taken to improve the functioning of different segments of the financial markets and thereby, to improve the operational effectiveness of monetary policy. The Liquidity Adjustment Facility (LAF), which was introduced in June 2000 has emerged as an effective and flexible instrument for managing liquidity on a day-to-day basis. In the second stage of the LAF, which commenced from May 2001, variable rate repo auctions replaced the collateralised lending facility and Level I support to primary dealers. Standing facilities were rationalised and a back-stop facility was introduced at variable market-related rates. Concurrently, LAF operating procedures were recast to improve operational flexibility and complementary measures were undertaken to improve the functioning of money and government securities market segments and to facilitate their orderly integration.

In order to enable the call money market to evolve into a pure inter-bank market, lending by non-banks was reduced to 85 per cent of their average daily call lending in 2000-01 from May 2001. The minimum maturity for wholesale term deposits of Rs.15 lakh and above has been reduced to 7 days from the earlier minimum maturity of 15 days. The maintenance of daily minimum cash reserve requirements has been lowered to 50 per cent from 65 per cent for the first seven days of the reporting fortnight. Interest paid on eligible balances under CRR has been raised to the level of the Bank Rate from November 3, 2001. The market has responded positively with an appreciable rise in turnover and a decline in volatility.

Several measures have also been taken to improve the functioning of the government securities market. 14-day and

182-day Treasury Bills were withdrawn and the notified amounts of 91-day Treasury Bills has been simultaneously increased. A Negotiated Dealing System (NDS) is being introduced to facilitate electronic bidding and to disseminate information on trades on a real-time basis. For this purpose, the Reserve Bank has begun the automation of its public debt offices. An important step is the setting up of the Clearing Corporation of India Ltd. (CCIL) to act as counterparty in all trades involving government securities, Treasury Bills, repos and foreign exchange. The entire system will operate in a networked environment and INdian FInancial NETwork (INFINET) will provide the backbone for communication.

A strong and resilient financial system and the orderly evolution of financial markets are key prerequisites for financial stability and economic progress. In keeping with the vision of an internationally competitive and sound banking system, deepening and broadening of prudential norms to the best internationally recognised standards have been the core of our approach to financial sector reforms. This has been supported concurrently by heightened market discipline, pro-active and comprehensive supervision of the financial system and the orderly development of financial market segments.

The calibration of the convergence with international standards is conditioned by the specific realities of our situation; however, the New Capital Accord of the Basel Committee on Banking Supervision which was released in January 2001 adds urgency to the process of convergence. It is against the backdrop of these exigencies that prudential norms are being constantly monitored and refined.

In the rec ent period, banks are being encouraged to build risk-weighted components of their subsidiaries into their own balance sheets and to assign additional capital. Risk weights are being constantly refined to take into recognition additional sources of risk. The concept of 'past due' in the identification of NPAs has been dispensed with. Banks and financial institutions are being urged to prepare to move to the international practice of the '90 day norm' in the classification of assets as non-performing by 2003-04.

The new Basel Accord, as contained in the second Consultative Paper on Capital Adequacy of the Basel Committee on Banking Supervision released in January 2001 is in response to the perceived rigidities in the 1988 Accord's capital requirements, the scope for capital arbitrage and the increased sophistication in the measurement and management of risk. The new Accord rests on three mutually reinforcing pillars i.e., minimum capital requirements, processes of supervisory review and market discipline. Under the first pillar, the current definition of capital and the minimum requirement of 8 per cent of capital to risk weighted assets is retained. Capital requirements would be extended on a consolidated basis to holding companies of banking groups.

The primary emphasis of the new Accord is on improving the measurement of risk. The process of measurement of market risk is maintained. Three alternatives for calculating credit risk capital requirements are proposed to be made available to banks, depending on the complexity of their business and the quality of their risk management operations.

The 'standardised approach' which can be employed by less complex banks remains conceptually the same as in the 1988 norms; however, it expands the scale of risk weights and uses external credit ratings to categorise credits. Banks with more advanced risk management capabilities can employ an internal ratings based (IRB) approach - 'foundation' and 'advanced' variants are proposed on a progression scale - in which banks may categorise exposures into multiple credit ratings of their approved internal rating systems. The internally estimated probability of default, the maturity of exposure and the credit type i.e., corporate or retail, will det ermine risk weights. There is a new explicit capital charge proposed on operational risk.

The processes of supervisory review contained in the second pillar emphasise the need for banks to develop sound internal procedures to assess the adequacy of capital based on a thorough evaluation of its risk profile and control environment, and to set commensurate targets for capital. The internal processes would be subject to supervisory evaluation, review and intervention, when appropriate.

The third pillar aims at bolstering market discipline through enhanced disclosure by banks. Disclosure requirements are set out in several areas under the new Accord, including the way in which banks calculate their capital adequacy and their risk assessment methods.

The Basel Committee on Banking Supervision has received more than 250 comments on the January 2001 proposals. The Committee is expected to release a fully specified proposal, based on these comments, in early 2002 and to finalise the Accord during 2002. An implementation date of 2005 is envisaged.

The Reserve Bank forwarded its comments to the Basel committee in May 2001. It has supported flexibility, discretion to national supervisors and a phased approach in implementing the Accord.

The Accord could initially apply to internationally active - banks with over 15 per cent of their business in cross-border transactions, as proposed by the Reserve Bank - and significant banks whose domestic market share exceeds 1 per cent - with a simplified standardised approach to be evolved for other banks. Material limits on cross-holdings of capital and eschewing of direct responsibility on external credit rating agencies in the assessment of bank assets have also been proposed by the Reserve Bank. It has also expressed its preference for external credit rating agencies that publicly disclose risk scores, rating processes and methodologies.

The new accord, when implemented, is likely to have significant implications for the banking system as a whole.

Besides requiring increased capital, it attaches urgency to the development of efficient and comprehensive internal systems for assessment and management of risks, setting up and adhering to adequate internal exposure limits and improving internal control generally.

The guidelines for risk management and asset liability management provided by the Reserve Bank serve as a useful foundation for building more sophisticated control systems.

The feedback received from few banks indicates the need for substantial upgradation of existing management information systems, risk management practices and technical skills.

Capital allocation is also expected to be more risk sensitive and, therefore, banks and financial institutions will have to plan in advance so that there are no disruptions in the capital structure. Further sophistication in risk management and control mechanisms will have to evolve as experience with preferential risk-weighting and sensitivity to external ratings is accumulated.

A key requirement when the new Accord, after further modification, becomes operational is that of high quality human resources to cope with and adapt to the new environment. Enhancing technical skills and abilities to handle new technologies and new risks, exploiting information flows to price them in, and developing foresight in anticipating changing risk-return relationships will become essential.

MARKET DISCIPLINE

Processes of transparency and market disclosure of critical information describing the risk profile, capital structure and capital adequacy are assuming increasing importance in the emerging environment.

Besides making banks more accountable and responsive to better-informed investors, these processes enable banks to strike the right balance between risks and rewards and to improve the access to markets. Improvements in market discipline also call for greater coordination between banks and regulators.

India has been a participant in the international initiatives to ensure improved processes of market discipline that are being worked out in several fora, such as, the multilateral organisations, the BIS, the Financial Stability Forum, and the Core Principles Liaison Group.

Concurrent efforts are underway to refine and upgrade financial information monitoring and flow, data dissemination and data warehousing.

Banks are currently required to disclose in their balance sheets information on maturity profiles of assets and liabilities, lending to sensitive sectors, movements in NPAs, besides providing information on capital, provisions, shareholdings of the government, value of investments in India and abroad, and other operating and profitability indicators.

Financial institutions are also required to meet these disclosure norms. Banks also have to disclose their total investments made in equity shares, units of mutual funds, bonds and debentures, and aggregate advances against shares in their notes to balance sheets.

From this year onwards, notes to banks' balance sheets will disclose the movement of provisions against NPAs as well as those held towards depreciation on investments. Guidelines relating to non-SLR investments through the private placement route mandate the disclosure of information on issuer composition and non-performing investments in a similar manner. Efforts have been made to identify and monitor early warning indicators of financial crises.

The overall approach is to combine the use of micro-prudential indicators with macro-economic indicators in order to develop a set of aggregate macro-prudential indicators. This brings about a mix between bottom-up and top-down assessment.

As the methodology gets refined and the indicators are stress-tested for predictive power, financial stability surveillance will be significantly improved. This process will involve greater transparency and objectivity in the disclosure practices of banks.

Efforts have also been made to set up a Credit Information Bureau to collect and share information on borrowers and improve the credit appraisal of banks and financial institutions within the ambit of the existing legislation.

The Bureau has been incorporated by the State Bank of India in collaboration with Housing Development Finance Corporation (HDFC) and foreign technology partners.

Collection and sharing of some items of information have already been initiated. Efforts are also going into the collection and sharing of information on private placement of debt under the Bureau so that there is greater transparency in such trades.

The possibility of collecting and disseminating information on suit-filed accounts by the Bureau (in place of the Reserve Bank) is being explored by a Working Group constituted for this purpose with representation from across the financial system. The Group will also examine the prospects of on-line supply of information and the processing of queries. A draft leg islation covering various aspects of information sharing, including issues relating to rights, responsibilities, and privacy has been prepared, which would considerably strengthen the functioning of the Bureau when it is enacted.

STANCE OF MONETARY POLICY FOR THE REMAINING PERIOD OF 2007-08

In April 2007, at the time of the Annual Policy Statement for 2007-08, global growth was expected to moderate and inflationary pressures were seen as persisting worldwide. With demand pressures having intensified in the domestic economy along with supply-side constraints, the Annual Policy Statement reiterated the stance set out in January 2007 of reinforcing the emphasis on price stability and well-anchored inflation expectations so as to enable continuation of the growth momentum. Credit quality and orderly financial markets were re-emphasised in conjunction with greater credit penetration and financial inclusion. The Annual Policy Statement also reaffirmed the resolve to respond swiftly with all possible measures to developments impinging on inflation expectations and the growth momentum. It was recognised that the likely evolution of macroeconomic and financial conditions indicates an environment supportive of sustaining the current growth momentum and that the Indian economy is possibly poised on the threshold of a step-up in the growth trajectory, but that there is evidence of some cyclical elements embedded in the structural change. Noting that the overarching policy challenge is to manage the transition to a higher growth path while containing inflationary pressures, the policy preference for the period ahead was indicated as strongly in favour of price stability and well-anchored inflation expectations with the endeavour being to contain inflation close to 5.0 per cent in 2007-08 and to the range of 4.0-4.5 per cent over the medium-term.

On a review, the prospects for growth in 2007-08 appear positive at the current juncture. The IMD has maintained its initial forecasts of rainfall at 93 per cent of the LPA for the country as a whole in the 2007 south-west monsoon season. Accordingly, by current indications, a return to trend growth in agriculture should be realisable. Growth in industrial and service sector activity, which constitute more than 80 per cent of the economy and contribute over 94 per cent of headline growth, is expected to be sustained, given the current momentum of expansion despite evolving uncertainties observed in recent weeks. Overall, for policy purposes, the projection of real GDP growth in 2007-08 at around 8.5 per cent, as set out in the Annual Policy Statement of April 2007, is retained, barring domestic or external shocks.

There are indications that the combination of lagged and cumulative effects of monetary policy actions and fiscal and administrative measures for supply management has had a salutary effect on inflation expectations, and headline inflation has turned benign in sharp contrast to the last quarter of 2006-07. Going forward, monetary management would need to be watchful of movements in commodity prices, particularly oil prices, the elevated levels of asset prices and the re-emergence of pricing power among producers as potential threats to inflation expectations. Assuming that aggregate supply management will continue to receive public policy attention and that a more active management of the capital account will be demonstrated, the outlook for inflation in 2007-08 remains unchanged. Accordingly, holding headline inflation within 5.0 per cent in 2007-08 assumes priority in the policy hierarchy; while reinforcing the medium-term objective to condition policy and perceptions to reduce inflation to 4.0-4.5 per cent on a sustained basis.

For the purpose of monetary policy formulation, the Annual Policy Statement of April 2007 projected the rate of money supply (M3) at around 17.0-17.5 per cent for 2007-08 in consonance with the outlook on growth and inflation. Consistent with the projections of money supply, the growth in aggregate deposits in 2007-08 was placed at around Rs.4,90,000 crore while non-food credit including investments in bonds/debentures/shares of public sector undertakings and private corporate sector and commercial paper (CP) was projected to decelerate to 24.0-25.0 per cent in 2007-08 from the average of 29.8 per cent over 2004-07. While non-food credit growth has decelerated, the acceleration in money supply and reserve money warrants an appropriate response.

Recent developments in the external sector indicate that the overall trade and current account deficits in 2007-08 are evolving as per expectations. However, net capital flows have been very strong so far in the current financial year. Early fiscal indicators suggest that the Centre's fiscal deficit is evolving as budgeted and is on course to meet the targets set in the Fiscal Responsibility and Budget Management (FRBM) Act, 2003.

By current reckoning, the global outlook is positive with continuing prospects for strong and stable growth but there are concerns about inflationary pressures worldwide. Monetary authorities are inclined to regard the current levels of real interest rates as warranting further withdrawal of monetary accommodation and are indicating a preparedness to respond to the manner in which the inflation scenario evolves. Financial markets have been aggressively re-pricing risks; however, the wide diffusion of risks and the abundance of liquidity has imparted considerable uncertainty. Visitations of volatility in equity and currency markets with worldwide ramifications have imparted an additional dimension of uncertainty to the evolution of the international economic environment. These developments are necessitating intensified policy monitoring with a policy preference for insulating domestic real activity from these shocks. Looking ahead, monetary policy in India would continue to be vigilant and pro-active in the context of any accentuation of global uncertainties that pose threats to growth and stability in the domestic economy.

The domestic outlook continues to be favourable and would dominate the dynamic setting of monetary policy in the period ahead.

It is important to design monetary policy such that it protects growth by contributing to the maintenance of stability. Accordingly, while the stance of monetary policy would continue to reinforce the emphasis on price stability and well-anchored inflation expectations and thereby sustain the growth momentum, contextually, financial stability may assume greater importance in the months to come.

Keeping the above in view, recent developments in financial markets in India and potential uncertainties in global markets warrant a higher priority for managing appropriate liquidity conditions in the policy hierarchy at the current juncture.

The Reserve Bank will continue with its policy of active demand management of liquidity through appropriate use of the CRR stipulations and open market operations (OMO) including the MSS and LAF, using all the policy instruments at its disposal flexibly, as and when the situation warrants.

In sum, barring the emergence of any adverse and unexpected developments in various sectors of the economy and keeping in view the current assessment of the economy including the outlook for inflation, the overall stance of monetary policy in the period ahead will broadly continue to be:

To reinforce the emphasis on price stability and well-anchored inflation expectations while ensuring a monetary and interest rate environment that supports export and investment demand in the economy so as to enable continuation of the growth momentum.

To re-emphasise credit quality and orderly conditions in financial markets for securing macroeconomic and, in particular, financial stability while simultaneously pursuing greater credit penetration and financial inclusion.

To respond swiftly with all possible measures as appropriate to the evolving global and domestic situation impinging on inflation expectations, financial stability and the growth momentum.

Monetary Measures

(a) Bank Rate

The Bank Rate has been kept unchanged at 6.0 per cent.

(b) Repo Rate/Reverse Repo Rate

The repo rate under the LAF is kept unchanged at 7.75 per cent.

The reverse repo rate under the LAF is kept unchanged at 6.0 per cent.

In view of the current macroeconomic and overall monetary and liquidity conditions, it has been decided to withdraw the ceiling of Rs. 3,000 crore on daily reverse repo under the LAF with effect from Monday, August 6, 2007. The Reserve Bank, however, retains the discretion to re-impose a ceiling as appropriate.

The Reserve Bank has the flexibility to conduct repo/reverse repo auctions at a fixed rate or at variable rates as circumstances warrant.

The Reserve Bank retains the option to conduct overnight or longer term repo/reverse repo under the LAF depending on market conditions and other relevant factors. The Reserve Bank will continue to use this flexibility including the right to accept or reject tender(s) under the LAF, wholly or partially, if deemed fit, so as to make efficient use of the LAF in daily liquidity management.

The second LAF, which was introduced from November 28, 2005 and is conducted between 3.00 p.m. and 3.45 p.m. on a daily basis, is withdrawn with effect from Monday, August 6, 2007.

(c) Cash Reserve Ratio

The cash reserve ratio (CRR) of scheduled banks is currently at 6.5 per cent. On a review of the current liquidity situation, it is considered desirable to increase the CRR by 50 basis points to 7.0 per cent with effect from the fortnight beginning August 4, 2007.

RBI ANNOUNCES VARIOUS MONETARY MEASURES INCLUDING INCREASE IN CRR

In the light of the current macroeconomic, monetary and anticipated liquidity conditions, and with a view to containing inflation expectations, Reserve Bank of India found it critical to take demonstrable and determined action on an urgent basis. Accordingly, the following monetary measures consistent with the stance of the monetary policy are announced by RBI:

(i) It has been decided to increase the fixed repo rate under the LAF by 25 basis points from 7.50 per cent to 7.75 per cent with immediate effect.

(ii) The other arrangements regarding the operations of LAF announced on March 2, 2007 will continue until further notice.

(iii) The policy of withdrawal of semi-durable and durable elements of liquidity through treasury bills and dated securities under MSS will continue. Accordingly, the Reserve Bank would, subject to variations in liquidity conditions, announce auctions of MSS covering issuances of treasury bills and dated securities on a weekly basis. The auction for Treasury bills under MSS would continue to take place by notifying the amounts under MSS every week along with the regular auction calendar as has been the existing practice. The Reserve Bank would retain the flexibility of reviewing the schedule of auctions under the MSS from time to time, in response to evolving circumstances.

(iv) The cash reserve ratio (CRR) of scheduled commercial banks (SCBs), regional rural banks (RRBs), scheduled co-operative banks and scheduled primary (urban) co-operative banks is being increased by one-half of one percentage point of their net demand and time liabilities (NDTL) in two stages, effective from the fortnights indicated below:

April 14, 2007 - 6.25, April 28, 2007 - 6.50

As a result of the above increase in the CRR, an amount of Rs.15,500 crore of resources of banks would be absorbed.

(v) The interest rate applicable on eligible CRR balances (i.e., the amount of reserves between the statutory minimum CRR and the CRR prescribed by the RBI) shall be reduced to 0.5 per cent per annum from the present 1.0 per cent per annum with effect from the fortnight beginning April 14, 2007.

In view of the following notable developments, Since the monetary measures that were announced on February 13, 2007, RBI has decided to announce new measures:

(a) The general index of industrial production increased by 11.0 per cent during April 2006 to January 2007 as against 8.0 per cent a year ago, as per the release of the Central Statistical Organisation (CSO) of March 12, 2007.

(b) Year-on-year inflation based on the wholesale price index (WPI), has ruled around 6.5 per cent for the third week in succession up to March 17, 2007 as per the data released today. At a disaggregated level, prices of primary articles, fuel group and manufactured products registered a year-on-year increase of 12.0 per cent, 1.0 per cent and 6.6 per cent as on March 17, 2007 as against 3.7 per cent, 8.9 per cent and 1.7 per cent a year ago.

(c) Inflation based on the consumer price index for industrial workers (CPI-IW), urban non-manual employees (CPI-UNME), agricultural labourers (CPI-AL) and rural labourers (CPI-RL) showed year-on-year increase to 7.6 per cent, 7.8 per cent, 9.8 per cent and 9.5 per cent in February 2007, respectively, from 5.0 per cent, 4.8 per cent and 5.0 per cent and 4.7 per cent, a year ago.

(d) The year-on-year growth in non-food bank credit of scheduled commercial banks (SCBs) was 29.5 per cent as on March 16, 2007 as against 32.7 per cent a year ago.

(e) The year-on-year growth in aggregate deposits of SCBs

was 24.8 per cent as on March 16, 2007, over and above 18.0 per cent a year ago.

(f) The year-on-year money supply (M3) growth up to March 16, 2007 was 22.0 per cent as against 16.9 per cent a year ago.

(g) Continuation of accelerated external inflows has resulted in accretion of US $ 18.6 billion to the foreign exchange reserves, taking their level from US $ 179.1 billion at the end of January, 2007 to US $ 197.7 billion on March 23, 2007.

(h) Additional liquidity amounting to Rs.23,894 crore was absorbed under the market stabilisation scheme (MSS) during February 1 - March 30, 2007.

(i) Globally, the process of withdrawal of accommodation in monetary policy is being vigorously pursued. Since mid-February, 2007 among the leading central banks, the European Central Bank and the Bank of Japan have raised key policy rates by 25 basis points each, while the People's Bank of China raised one year lending rates by 27 basis points and the reserve requirements by 50 basis points. There has been no change in the policy rates of the US Federal Reserve, the Bank of England, the Bank of Canada, the Reserve Bank of Australia and the Reserve Bank of New Zealand all of which had undertaken prior policy action.

Use of Liquidity Adjustment Facility (LAF) for On-lending

There have been some enquiries regarding RBI's indication that, inter-alia, resources accessed from the Reserve Bank's LAF window should not be used for on-lending by banks.

In this context, RBI has clarified that the intent of this advice is that the recourse to LAF by market participants should not be persistent in order to fund balance sheets for credit needs of customers, but banks can utilize the funds borrowed under this facility for inter-bank lending. Such, inter-bank lending is part of normal money market functioning that enables daily liquidity management by market participants having temporary mismatches.

RBI ANNOUNCE MODIFIED ARRANGEMENTS FOR LAF AND MSS TO MANAGE LIQUIDITY

In the Third Quarter Review of Annual Statement on Monetary Policy for the Year 2006-07, the Reserve Bank had stated that, 'over the remaining part of the year, management of liquidity would receive priority in the policy hierarchy' (Paragraph 89). It was also stated that, 'the Reserve Bank retains the option to conduct overnight repo or longer term repo under LAF depending on market conditions and other relevant factors. The Reserve Bank will continue to use this flexibility including the right to accept or reject tender(s) under the LAF, wholly or partially, if deemed fit, so as to make efficient use of LAF in daily liquidity management' (paragraph 95).

Existing Arrangements

The Reserve Bank has been currently conducting liquidity management largely through the Liquidity Adjustment Facility (LAF), which is intended as a window for adjusting day-to-day liquidity mismatches, and the Market Stabilisation Scheme (MSS), which is used for addressing large swings in liquidity conditions which could have a more durable character.

Under the existing MSS programme being conducted in accordance with the annual ceiling for 2006-07 fixed at Rs.70,000 crore, the issuance of Treasury bills under MSS has been undertaken through regular weekly auctions with an MSS portion of 91-day Treasury Bills of Rs.1,500 crore and those for the fortnightly 182-day and 364-day Treasury bills of Rs.1,000 crore each. While announcing the resumption of MSS T-bills programme as above, it was stated that the Reserve Bank would retain the flexibility of reviewing the auctions under the

MSS from time to time, in response to evolving circumstances. Under the existing MSS programme, an amount of Rs.16,457 crore has been sterilised in the current financial year so far, of which Rs.14,341 crore has been in the first half of 2006-07. The outstandings under MSS as of today is Rs.45,457 crore.

The LAF has switched to a significant surplus mode with substantial net absorptions being made in recent days. Under the existing arrangements, the LAF absorbs any excess liquidity offered by scheduled commercial banks (excluding RRBs) and primary dealers at a fixed rate. However, the Reserve Bank has always maintained that banks should use the LAF window for equilibrating very short term mismatches over temporary periods.

MSS - Modified Arrangements

On a review of the liquidity conditions, RBI has decided on 2nd March 2007, that the MSS will now use a mix of Treasury bills and dated securities in a more flexible manner keeping in view the capital flows in the recent period, the assessment of volatility and durability of capital flows, and the paramount importance attached to liquidity management in containing inflation. The Reserve Bank would, subject to variations in liquidity, announce every Friday the possibility and the quantum of MSS issuances for the succeeding week. These announcements would cover issuances of Treasury Bills and dated securities under MSS. Their auctions would be conducted in accordance with provisions of Memorandum of Understanding between the Reserve Bank of India and the Government of India dated March 25, 2004 under which Reserve Bank and the Government of India agree on an annual ceiling and the Reserve Bank decides the amount, tenor, modalities and the timing of issue.

The auction for Treasury bills under MSS would continue to take place by notifying the amounts under MSS every week along with the regular auction calendar as has been the existing practice. The Reserve Bank would retain the flexibility of reviewing the schedule of auctions under the MSS from time to time, in response to evolving circumstances.

LAF - Modified Arrangements

On a review of the liquidity conditions, it has been decided that in view of the enhanced MSS programme being put in place and the need to restore LAF as a facility for equilibrating very short-term mismatches, the Reserve Bank would modulate the liquidity it absorbs through the daily reverse repo auctions.

Accordingly, starting March 5, 2007 (Monday), daily reverse repo absorptions would be limited to a maximum of Rs.3,000 crore each day comprising Rs.2,000 crore in the First LAF and Rs. 1,000 crore in the Second LAF. In case of partial rejection of bids, allocations would normally be made proportionately on a pro-rata basis. While bidding in LAF auctions, scheduled commercial banks (excluding RRBs) and primary dealers should ensure that clear funds are available with them to cover the bid at the time of its submission.

The above modified arrangements for LAF and MSS being put in place are expected to facilitate the maintenance of appropriate liquidity in the system and to respond more swiftly to the evolving liquidity situation in line with the objectives and stance of the monetary policy.

USE OF LIQUIDITY ADJUSTMENT FACILITY (LAF) FOR ON-LENDING

There have been some enquiries regarding RBI's indication that, inter-alia, resources accessed from the Reserve Bank's LAF window should not be used for on-lending by banks.

In this context, RBI has clarified that the intent of this advice is that the recourse to LAF by market participants should not be persistent in order to fund balance sheets for credit needs of customers, but banks can utilize the funds borrowed under this facility for inter-bank lending.

Such, inter-bank lending is part of normal money market functioning that enables daily liquidity management by market participants having temporary mismatches.

RBI ANNOUNCE MODIFIED ARRANGEMENTS FOR LAF AND MSS TO MANAGE LIQUIDITY

In the Third Quarter Review of Annual Statement on Monetary Policy for the Year 2006-07, the Reserve Bank had stated that, 'over the remaining part of the year, management of liquidity would receive priority in the policy hierarchy' (Paragraph 89).

It was also stated that, 'the Reserve Bank retains the option to conduct overnight repo or longer term repo under LAF depending on market conditions and other relevant factors. The Reserve Bank will continue to use this flexibility including the right to accept or reject tender(s) under the LAF, wholly or partially, if deemed fit, so as to make efficient use of LAF in daily liquidity management' (paragraph 95).

Existing Arrangements

The Reserve Bank has been currently conducting liquidity management largely through the Liquidity Adjustment Facility (LAF), which is intended as a window for adjusting day-to-day liquidity mismatches, and the Market Stabilisation Scheme (MSS), which is used for addressing large swings in liquidity conditions which could have a more durable character.

Under the existing MSS programme being conducted in accordance with the annual ceiling for 2006-07 fixed at Rs.70,000 crore, the issuance of Treasury bills under MSS has been undertaken through regular weekly auctions with an MSS portion of 91-day Treasury Bills of Rs.1,500 crore and those for the fortnightly 182-day and 364-day Treasury bills of Rs.1,000 crore each.

While announcing the resumption of MSS T-bills

programme as above, it was stated that the Reserve Bank would retain the flexibility of reviewing the auctions under the MSS from time to time, in response to evolving circumstances. Under the existing MSS programme, an amount of Rs.16,457 crore has been sterilised in the current financial year so far, of which Rs.14,341 crore has been in the first half of 2006-07. The outstandings under MSS as of today is Rs.45,457 crore.

The LAF has switched to a significant surplus mode with substantial net absorptions being made in recent days. Under the existing arrangements, the LAF absorbs any excess liquidity offered by scheduled commercial banks (excluding RRBs) and primary dealers at a fixed rate.

However, the Reserve Bank has always maintained that banks should use the LAF window for equilibrating very short term mismatches over temporary periods.

MSS - Modified Arrangements

On a review of the liquidity conditions, RBI has decided on 2nd March 2007, that the MSS will now use a mix of Treasury bills and dated securities in a more flexible manner keeping in view the capital flows in the recent period, the assessment of volatility and durability of capital flows, and the paramount importance attached to liquidity management in containing inflation.

The Reserve Bank would, subject to variations in liquidity, announce every Friday the possibility and the quantum of MSS issuances for the succeeding week. These announcements would cover issuances of Treasury Bills and dated securities under MSS.

Their auctions would be conducted in accordance with provisions of Memorandum of Understanding between the Reserve Bank of India and the Government of India dated March 25, 2004 under which Reserve Bank and the Government of India agree on an annual ceiling and the Reserve Bank decides the amount, tenor, modalities and the timing of issue.

The auction for Treasury bills under MSS would continue to take place by notifying the amounts under MSS every week along with the regular auction calendar as has been the existing practice.

The Reserve Bank would retain the flexibility of reviewing the schedule of auctions under the MSS from time to time, in response to evolving circumstances.

LAF - Modified Arrangements

On a review of the liquidity conditions, it has been decided that in view of the enhanced MSS programme being put in place and the need to restore LAF as a facility for equilibrating very short-term mismatches, the Reserve Bank would modulate the liquidity it absorbs through the daily reverse repo auctions.

Accordingly, starting March 5, 2007 (Monday), daily reverse repo absorptions would be limited to a maximum of Rs.3,000 crore each day comprising Rs.2,000 crore in the First LAF and Rs. 1,000 crore in the Second LAF. In case of partial rejection of bids, allocations would normally be made proportionately on a pro-rata basis.

While bidding in LAF auctions, scheduled commercial banks (excluding RRBs) and primary dealers should ensure that clear funds are available with them to cover the bid at the time of its submission.

The above modified arrangements for LAF and MSS being put in place are expected to facilitate the maintenance of appropriate liquidity in the system and to respond more swiftly to the evolving liquidity situation in line with the objectives and stance of the monetary policy.

CRITICISM OF FRACTIONAL-RESERVE BANKING

The primary criticisms relate to the potential fragility of bank liquidity in a fractional reserve banking environment, the financial risk of bank runs that depositors bear when depositing money with banks, and the impact that demand deposits have on the stock of money, and on inflation (that is, the implicit debasement of the currency and its associated impact on the exchange rate). An alternative to fractional reserve banking is making the practice illegal and classifying the practice as a form of embezzlement, only permitting full-reserve banking. With full-reserve banking, some monetary reformers as such as Stephen Zarlenga of the American Monetary Institute, support the concurrent issuance of debt-free fiat currency from the Treasury, while others such as Congressman Ron Paul and the Ludwig von Mises Institute call for a commodity currency such as was possible under the Gold Standard.

The reserve banking, by expanding the money supply, will lower the interest rates compared to a hypothetical full-reserve banking system. They argue that this will affect the role of the interest rate as the price of investment capital, guiding investment decisions. In their view, the natural (free of government influence) interest rate reflects the actual time preference of lenders and borrowers.

Government's monopolistic control of the money supply through central banks and regulations insuring fractional-reserve banking activities disturbs this equilibrium such that the interest rate no longer reflects the real supply of and demand for investment capital. If the interest rate is artificially low, then the demand for loans will be higher than the actual supply of willing lenders, and if the interest rate is artificially high, the opposite situation will occur.

This misinformation leads investors to misallocate capital, borrowing and investing either too much or too little in long-term projects. Periodic recessions, then, are seen as necessary "corrections" following periods of fiat credit expansion, when unprofitable investments stimulated by fiat credit creation are liquidated, freeing capital for new sustainable investment. One of the proponents of aspects of the business cycle theory, Friedrich von Hayek, was awarded the Nobel Prize in

Economics,, although Hayek himself accepted that bank credit and fractional reserve banking - even if they contributed to business cycles - were necessary as "the price we pay for a speed of development exceeding" that which would otherwise be possible, and that "financial institutions have never been prohibited from holding fractional reserves. A full-reserve banking system should not be enforced legally and dispute Murray Rothbard's characterization of fractional-reserve banking as a simple form of recursive embezzlement, and rather advocate the abolition of central banking and suggest that free banking replace the current system.

Fractional reserve banking involves the issuance and creation of commercial bank money, which increases the money supply on an exponential basis. According to the quantity theory of money, this increase in the money supply leads to more money "chasing" the same amount of goods, which leads to inflation. The exchange rate or purchasing power of the monetary unit is governed by the quantity of money, including demand deposits and notes, and therefore view fractional reserve banking as a cause of inflation.

Some quantity theorists who criticize fractional reserve banking support minimum reserve ratios or other government controls on the quantity of money created by commercial banks. Some support a gold standard or silver standard to restrain "unfettered", "speculative" fractional-reserve banking activities. Fractional reserve currency has also been characterized as a hybrid of receipt currency and fiat currency, and a form of currency that will eventually become fiat currency.

RBI ANNOUNCE MODIFIED ARRANGEMENTS FOR LAF AND MSS TO MANAGE LIQUIDITY

In the Third Quarter Review of Annual Statement on Monetary Policy for the Year 2006-07, the Reserve Bank had stated that, 'over the remaining part of the year, management of liquidity would receive priority in the policy hierarchy'.

It was also stated that, 'the Reserve Bank retains the option to conduct overnight repo or longer term repo under LAF depending on market conditions and other relevant factors. The Reserve Bank will continue to use this flexibility including the right to accept or reject tender(s) under the LAF, wholly or partially, if deemed fit, so as to make efficient use of LAF in daily liquidity management'.

MSS - Modified Arrangements

On a review of the liquidity conditions, RBI has decided on 2nd March 2007, that the MSS will now use a mix of Treasury bills and dated securities in a more flexible manner keeping in view the capital flows in the recent period, the assessment of volatility and durability of capital flows, and the paramount importance attached to liquidity management in containing inflation.

The Reserve Bank would, subject to variations in liquidity, announce every Friday the possibility and the quantum of MSS issuances for the succeeding week. These announcements would cover issuances of Treasury Bills and dated securities under MSS.

Their auctions would be conducted in accordance with provisions of Memorandum of Understanding between the Reserve Bank of India and the Government of India dated March 25, 2004 under which Reserve Bank and the Government of India agree on an annual ceiling and the Reserve Bank decides the amount, tenor, modalities and the timing of issue.

The auction for Treasury bills under MSS would continue to take place by notifying the amounts under MSS every week along with the regular auction calendar as has been the existing practice. The Reserve Bank would retain the flexibility of reviewing the schedule of auctions under the MSS from time to time, in response to evolving circumstances.

LAF - Modified Arrangements

On a review of the liquidity conditions, it has been decided that in view of the enhanced MSS programme being put in place and the need to restore LAF as a facility for equilibrating very short-term mismatches, the Reserve Bank would modulate the liquidity it absorbs through the daily reverse repo auctions.

Accordingly, starting March 5, 2007 (Monday), daily reverse repo absorptions would be limited to a maximum of Rs.3,000 crore each day comprising Rs.2,000 crore in the First LAF and Rs. 1,000 crore in the Second LAF. In case of partial rejection of bids, allocations would normally be made proportionately on a pro-rata basis.

While bidding in LAF auctions, scheduled commercial banks (excluding RRBs) and primary dealers should ensure that clear funds are available with them to cover the bid at the time of its submission.

The above modified arrangements for LAF and MSS being put in place are expected to facilitate the maintenance of appropriate liquidity in the system and to respond more swiftly to the evolving liquidity situation in line with the objectives and stance of the monetary policy.

Existing Arrangements

The Reserve Bank has been currently conducting liquidity management largely through the Liquidity Adjustment Facility (LAF), which is intended as a window for adjusting day-to-day liquidity mismatches, and the Market Stabilisation Scheme (MSS), which is used for addressing large swings in liquidity conditions which could have a more durable character.

Under the existing MSS programme being conducted in accordance with the annual ceiling for 2006-07 fixed at Rs.70,000 crore, the issuance of Treasury bills under MSS has been undertaken through regular weekly auctions with an MSS portion of 91-day Treasury Bills of Rs.1,500 crore and those for the fortnightly 182-day and 364-day Treasury bills of Rs.1,000 crore each.

While announcing the resumption of MSS T-bills programme as above, it was stated that the Reserve Bank would retain the flexibility of reviewing the auctions under the MSS from time to time, in response to evolving circumstances.

Under the existing MSS programme, an amount of Rs.16,457 crore has been sterilised in the current financial year so far, of which Rs.14,341 crore has been in the first half of 2006-07. The outstandings under MSS as of today is Rs.45,457 crore.

The LAF has switched to a significant surplus mode with substantial net absorptions being made in recent days. Under the existing arrangements, the LAF absorbs any excess liquidity offered by scheduled commercial banks (excluding RRBs) and primary dealers at a fixed rate. However, the Reserve Bank has always maintained that banks should use the LAF window for equilibrating very short term mismatches over temporary periods.

Bibliography

Besley, T.: *How do Merket Failures Justify Interventions in Rural Credit Markets?*, Washington, D. C., World Bank, 1994

Bouman, F.J.A.: *Small, Short and Unsecured: Informal Rural Finance in India*, Delhi, Oxford University Press, 1989.

Cavanagh, John, and Mander, Jerry: *Alternatives to Economic Globalization : A Better World Is Possible*, San Francisco, CA : Berrett-Koehler, 2004.

Dhingra, C.: *The Indian Economy: Resources, Planning, Development, and Problems*, Delhi, Sultan Chand, 1983.

Eleanor B. Steinberg and Joseph A. Yager: *New Means of Financing International Needs: Possible Sources of Finance*, Washington D.C.: The Brookings Institution, 1978.

Ferraro, Gary P.: *The Cultural Dimension of International Business*, Englewood Cliffs, Prentice Hall, 1997.

Goldsmith, W.: *The Financial Development of India, 1860-1977*, New Haven, Yale University Press, 1983.

Guhan, S.: *The World Bank's Lending in South Asia*, Washington, Brookings Institution, 1995.

Le Prestre, Philippe: *The World Bank and the Environmental Challenge*, London, Associated University Presses, 1989.

Magliveras, Konstantinos D. *Banks, Fraud and Crime*, Lloyd's of London Press, London, 2000.

Mowlana, H.: *Global Information and World Communication: New Frontiers in International Relations*, London, Sage Publications, 1997.

Musalem, Errico, Luca & Alberto: *Offshore Banking: An Analysis of Micro-and Macro-Prudential Issues*, IMF, Washington, D.C., 1999.

Pettifor, Ann: *Real World Economic Outlook: The Legacy of Globalization: Debt and Deflation*, New York, Palgrave MacMillan, 2003.

Ranade, Sudhanshu: *Rural Banking Adrift*, Bombay, Jaico Publishing House, 1984.

Index

□□□